All Wound Up

the
yarn harlot
writes
for a spin

stephanie pearl-mcphee

Andrews McMeel
Publishing, LLC
Kansas City • Sydney • London

Andrews McMeel Publishing, LLC
an Andrews McMeel Universal company
1130 Walnut Street, Kansas City, Missouri 64106

www.andrewsmcmeel.com

11 12 13 14 15 RR2 10 9 8 7 6 5 4 3 2 1

ISBN: 978-0-7407-9757-6

Library of Congress Control Number: 2010921939

Cover design by Erica Becker

ATTENTION: SCHOOLS AND BUSINESSES

Andrews McMeel books are available at quantity discounts with bulk purchase for educational, business, or sales promotional use. For information, please e-mail the Andrews McMeel Publishing Special Sales Department:
specialsales@amuniversal.com

CONTENTS

THIS ISN'T WORKING

Sitting in an office, not too long ago, I was knitting away while I waited my turn. There was a woman opposite me, about my age and station, who was waiting as well—or I should say "was waiting also," because she really wasn't waiting well at all. While I worked, turning useless wait time into a few inches of a sleeve, she rotated through a series of activities that included complaining, pacing, flipping through magazines, and, finally, sighing frequently and loudly. I've mothered three teenaged girls. I'm used to a flounce, a flop, and a sigh actually meaning that someone wants to talk, so when we got to the sixty-seventh sigh, I caught on that it might be a form of communication. "The wait's getting to you?" I asked, smiling and continuing to knit.

"It really is!" the woman exclaimed, while slamming another elderly magazine back onto the table. "This wait is way past stupid," she pouted, then rearranged her hands in her lap again, wringing them briefly, and then finally crossing them across her chest. "You have a lot of patience," she said, looking at my knitting.

"I don't really," I replied, glancing at my chart and then back at my knitting. "I'd be out of my mind if I didn't have something to do. The knitting really helps me be patient. Without it I'd have harassed the receptionist or rifled your purse for something interesting by now." We laughed and chatted for a few minutes. She asked me what I was making, if it was hard, and whether it took me long to learn—all the standard questions—and then slouched in her chair, trying to be civil despite the fact that we'd been trapped in a government office for so long that we were visibly aging. Eventually she leaned forward, looked at my knitting, and said, "It looks like fun. I wish I had time to knit, but I'm just too busy."

There it was. That sentence. The one that puts me right over the top. The one for which I've yet to figure out a snappy comeback. Every time someone tells me that they don't have time to knit, I come almost publicly undone—and it happens all the time. I can handle it when people say it might be too fiddly for them. I point out that it's child labor in much of the world and that if a kid can do it, so can they. I can handle it when they tell me that they don't think they're smart enough. I repeat the child labor thing and point out that it's really only two stitches, knit and purl, and that if they're smart enough to read and write, a system with twenty-six movements and pieces of code, they should be able to manage a system with only two. If all else fails and they still look at me with doubt, or imply that I, as a knitter, possess more general skills than they do, then I point out that there are whole societies where everyone knits, and this means that it can't be a skill that only a few genius souls can do. Anyone can knit, I tell them. A few people show a lot of talent for it, and they'll knit better, but really, knitting is far easier than being literate, and our cultural expectation is that almost everyone be able to read.

Those thoughts I understand, and I can talk with people about them without feeling anything other than a profound sense of boredom at the repetition. People honestly don't know anything about knitting; it looks way trickier than it is, and they don't think about how many smart things they already do each day and what that likely means for their general ability to manage string with a couple of sticks. I can handle being a walking public service announcement right up until someone says, "I wish I had time to knit," and then the purple creeping rage starts to seep in, usually because the person who has just said this to me is almost always doing what I'm doing. This lady and I were both sitting in the office waiting room for almost an hour. I was knitting, she was sitting there, and she says she wishes she had time to knit? It was all I could do not to scream, "Newsflash! You have time right now, just like me!" but I didn't, mostly because I think it would have been awkward after that, and I didn't know how much longer I'd be trapped with her. We fell into an uncomfortable silence, me slightly pissed off, her with no idea why. I knitted. She sat. I thought.

I know the lady probably didn't mean to be disrespectful, and certainly didn't intend for me to spend as much time thinking about the words "I wish I had time to knit" as I am now, but really, what was she saying? All I could hear is that because I was knitting she perceived that I had more time than she did, even though we both appeared to have the same amount of time available to us. If I had told her that I knit for several hours a day (which I didn't—I thought I was in deep enough already) I could perhaps have understood it, but really, for all this lady knew, I only knit in government waiting rooms. Had I told her that I knit for several hours a day, she probably would have been absolutely gobsmacked at the huge amounts of time that I must have available to me.

This woman was—or at least knew—someone who spent a lot of time just sitting passively in front of a screen, riding the subway, waiting in line, or being put on hold. In fact, she was almost certainly going home to plunk herself down on the couch to watch back-to-back episodes of *America's Next Top Model*. She must have understood the concept of waiting or sitting idly for hours on end, but having something productive to fill all that idle time? She couldn't understand that. She was reduced to saying, "I wish I had time to knit." How did doing something productive become a symbol of having idle time, while being idle is seen as having no time? What's driving that perception, and am I the only one who is confused by it?

A couple of months ago I was knitting on the bus, and a lady (who was, by the way, just sitting there, without even a book or anything—it boggles the mind) did the whole knitting quiz thing with me. She asked what I was doing, what I was making, and, after I told her it was knitting and I was making socks, she asked how long it took to knit a pair of socks. I said it depended on a lot of things, but it took me about sixteen hours for a pair. Her eyes bugged out of her head, and then she shook her head at me like becoming a knitter was now completely out of the question. If it was going to take actual time to knit things—you know, time that she could use to sit on the bus doing absolutely nothing—then she couldn't relate to it at all. She shrugged her shoulders, looked at me like I was the biggest wingnut she'd ever come upon on a public transit system (which I'm totally not, I assure you), and said, "Well. It must be nice to have that kind of time."

Nice to have that kind of time? What kind of time are we talking about here? She was talking as if we had different sorts of time, but near as I could tell, I was on the bus and she was on the bus. I was knitting and churning out a sock, while she was sitting there doing an impression of a rock, and somehow I was the one who had a bucket of free time? That wasn't the only thing: That lady had a tone, and it was a tone I hear all the time. It was the tone that says that if you have enough time to knit a sock, then you must be heading to a joyless, empty home, devoid of all interest and companionship and comforted only by cats. (For the record, I do have a cat, but I bet that woman does, too.)

It is mind boggling to me that, in a culture where the average person spends four hours a day watching TV, knitting is perceived as doing less than nothing. Knitting is obviously productive. It's making something, like woodworking or cooking. You can prove it by waving around a bunch of sweaters and half a hat you whacked out in one morning while converting useless time into clothing, and still for some insane reason, that actual production, which is no different than building a bookcase, is seen as an indicator that you have time, or sometimes even that you are wasting time. Bizarrely, this happens even though knitting has lots in common with other activities that we don't think of as wasteful—and it is even more productive than lots of other things that are normalized entirely, like watching television while you sit as inert as dirt. I think about this all the time. How did the world around us develop this attitude?

I've wondered if it's because of how far removed most people are from the clothes they need. Not so long ago, at least relative to human history, knitting was seen as work. If you needed a pair of mittens, you either had to knit them or had to pay someone to knit them for you, but either way someone sitting and knitting certainly wasn't seen as wasting time. They were either producing an item that they needed for their family or contributing to their family's economy. Enter the Industrial Revolution, and mitten making started being done by machines. In no time at all, we've managed to become such a consumeristic, product-driven society that people have stopped thinking that it's a waste to buy something you could make yourself and started thinking that it's wasteful to make something you could be buying. All of our emphasis shifted to the exchange of cash for products, and maybe mitten making now isn't worth the time. Is it because there's a perception that the mittens we're getting aren't really made? That they just spring into being and so knitting mittens seems bonkers when you can simply buy the ones that grow on trees? I try to break it down, but it's just such a crazy argument: "I don't want to waste time making mittens; I want to spend time buying them."

Sometimes I wonder whether knitting, despite being really productive, doesn't *look* productive to nonknitters. Knitting looks relaxing (at least once you're past the initial sweating, staring, and swearing phase). It looks peaceful, restful, pleasant, and calming, and you know what? It is all of those things. A whole lot of knitters (myself included) knit because it makes us better people. Way better people. Without my knitting, I have a lot of trouble even being polite to great swathes of humanity, never mind being relaxed about it. When we sit there, knitting away, we're having a grand time, and while we know it's an intricate activity that's great for our brains, to the uninitiated it may not look like we're doing much. Well, not much except, at its best, a complex, repetitive, visual, spatial task that develops hand–eye coordination, enhances neural connectivity, and uses both hemispheres of the brain at once. That's all, but people can't see that, and maybe because we look like we're relaxing they think we have all this time on our hands. No, wait. It can't be that, or popping a DVD in the player and lying on the couch wouldn't be considered a better way to spend time by so many people.

Perhaps it's simple defensiveness. Perhaps the people who say "I don't have the time" are trying to justify their own slacker ways. Maybe, just maybe, when they see me using my time to churn something out while they're just sitting there, some little voice in the back of their head is judging them. Perhaps, there is the briefest flash of insight, as my hands move and theirs don't, as I make something and they don't, as my time is spent and theirs is wasted, and they have a creeping little feeling deep down inside—a feeling that they don't quite know how to identify, a feeling that's super complex. Out of nowhere, out of the depths of their very souls, perhaps a little resonant voice says, "Well, look at that. That looks more interesting than just sitting here; we should knit too. Wouldn't it be nice to be productive? Isn't there something wrong with a life that has this much idleness in it? Aren't we colossally bored by it all?" When that happens, I think the regular part of their brain panics, because it's starting to look like the status quo is getting questioned, and that part of the personality in question—that part that likes things the way they are and loves stereotypes and embraces consumerism and sees no joy in work—picks up a metaphoric big stick and says the only thing that it can say in the face of an uprising. It says, "No, we can't knit. We're not smart enough, we don't know how, learning something new is scary . . . and besides . . . we, um . . . we don't have time! We're too busy. Yeah, that's it. With that, the idleness of a modern life is sanctified, most people slip back into compliant waiting and watching, saving time by buying what they need, confident that it would be a waste of time to make it, understanding that only grandmothers and terrifically boring people knit, and that if they knit like I did, sitting here in a government office, watching each other's hair grow, it would be curtains for any sort of social life that they may have hoped for themselves.

It has to be that, I tell myself, as I fill empty time with action. It has to be, because the alternative is that a whole lot of people have started thinking sideways, and that we live in a culture suddenly chock full of people who think that this simple, productive work that I'm doing is a sign that I don't have enough real work to fill my hours, that the way I've chosen to fill idle moments is a sign that I am, indeed, more idle than they are, and that, for the record, watching TV with a bag of chips in your hand would be a lot more valid, a lot easier to understand, than choosing not to just sit here.

That has to be it. I'm sure of it.

JANUARY

*I*t is January. January means, here in Ontario, Canada, that things are cold. Not the sort of cold that's an interesting footnote to the way that Mother Nature does things, but cold in the way that can kill people if they aren't careful. It is cold that freezes the hairs in your nose the minute you take a breath, cold that makes your hands hurt and your feet ache. Cold that can cancel school, even without a snow day, because it isn't safe to be outside long enough to walk there or even to wait for the bus. It is crazy, stupid cold that makes the snow squeak and the air sparkle, and it isn't even "really cold" compared to other places in Canada. On this night, it is about –20° C / –4° F, and to go to the store I'm wearing my store-bought parka but have added handknit socks, a vest, a sweater, a hat, leg warmers, wristers, a scarf, and two pairs of mittens. Clad as I am, in handknits from head to toe, I trudge through the snow and cold, and I imagine that other people are looking at me and wishing that they could be me. I feel sure that they too wish that they were a knitter with the intelligence and skill to fortify themselves against the

Canadian winter. They had to cop out and go to the store for their mittens, but look at me! Clearly, in any honest war against winter, I would be heralded as the winner. This is what I imagine they are thinking when they see me. In reality, they're probably wondering why that crazy lady looks so proud to be wearing so much mismatched clothing . . . but they're missing the point.

This cold is hard to explain to knitters who live in other places. It's something that I struggle to explain to many of my friends in the United States. Almost all of your country, I remind them, is south of here. I know it gets cold in a great many places there. I have compared notes with knitters in Wisconsin and been satisfied that they know the kind of cold I'm talking about, but that's just my point. That conversation only happens between one person who lives in the southernmost part of her country (me) and a knitter who lives in the northernmost part of theirs. Move a little bit in either direction and we have little to discuss. What gets lost, once you move out of that really narrow geographic point of comparison, is that this is the sort of cold that doesn't suffer any fools. This sort of cold means that it matters if your car breaks down on a back road or if you lose your house keys. Here, it matters if you are wearing your mittens.

A few years ago, when I was on a book deadline, a friend let me stay at their cabin. It was north of here, and it was isolated. It was more than a kilometer to the deserted road, and that kilometer wasn't plowed, so the way in and out was by hiking, with snowshoes and a sled to pull your things on if you were lucky, and an exhausting trudge through the snow if you weren't. (If you live in one of those aforementioned southern places, you might not have ever experienced a sincere desire for snowshoes. Walking through deep snow is exhausting— like walking through water. It adds resistance at best, and obstruction at worst. As in water, one cannot run in deep snow. Snowshoes mean that you walk on snow, rather than through it. They are a miracle.) This place was so far out in the middle of nowhere, and the Canadian winter so cold, that I was advised that if something went wrong, I should not hike out for help. It was around −30° C / −22° F when I got there, and that means that exposed skin can freeze (read: frostbite) in less than twenty minutes. In that sort of cold, no matter how quickly I walked, the cold would get me before I got to people. Being the sort of person who plans for emergencies, I asked what I should do if I were in trouble—if I couldn't go for help, and I was there alone, what exactly was to be my plan? The gentleman I asked cocked his head and laughed. "Be smart," he said. "Don't get into trouble."

I took that to heart, but the woods around the place were beautiful, and I wanted to walk in them. I decided to be smart. The cabin was in a part of Ontario that is on the Canadian Shield. That means that everywhere you go there are huge shelves, cracks, and chunks of Precambrian rock. It's dangerous to walk on in the summer if you're not careful, but in the winter it takes some extra intellect, since the snow covers the rock and you can't see what dangers lurk beneath. There are ways around this, though, and if you're smart, you're safe. I decided to brave it. I headed out, warm and cozy in layers of alpaca and wool, and glanced at my watch as I left. At −30° C I had about twenty minutes to walk before I needed to worry. From the cabin I could see a ridge that overlooked the river, and I made that my goal.

The way to walk on shield rock in the snow is to follow deer track. The deer know their way around, and they live there all year round. If you walk where they walk, then you know that you won't fall, because they haven't. (Similarly, a place where the deer won't walk should be avoided, and a frozen deer lying in your path can only be interpreted as a bad sign.) I was walking along, stepping in the footsteps of the deer who had walked before me, when I got to a place where the deer I was following had taken a long stride, and I (with my legs that are not quite as long as a deer's) stepped between her hoofprints.

Instantly, my leg shot down into a crack in the rock, and in the beat of a heart I'd thrown myself forward to lie down (just as you should if you fall through the ice) and stopped falling. I crawled forward, out of the crack that had nearly claimed my life. When my heart had stopped pounding, I looked back at what I was sure would be a cliff that had been revealed by falling snow and avalanche, and felt immediately stupid. It wasn't a big crack at all. I sat there for just a few minutes, gathering myself and looking back at the deer track. There, right before the crack, were two deer prints exactly side by side. That's not a step. That's a jump. The deer, in her infinite wisdom, had jumped over the crack she knew was there, and I had failed to notice. That wasn't smart. I could have easily broken an ankle or gotten my foot caught, which is a bonehead move at the best of times but could be deadly in temperatures like this.

I picked myself up and brushed most of the snow off so I didn't get colder faster, and I started to walk back to the house, following the deer track precisely, stepping exactly where they had stepped. Back in the house I made tea and knit for a bit while I watched night come, and I thought about what it's like to be isolated in weather like this. I could see how it would be pretty easy to kill yourself just by getting lost. I'm sure that given an unlimited amount of time I could always find my way back to the cabin, but when it's cold you don't have an unlimited amount of time to apply your intellect to the problem. If I got lost up here I'd have twenty minutes to solve the thing. After that it could cost me a toe or two—or worse. If you're not smart enough to realize that there's no way to really get the upper hand on nature, then natural selection is going to take you out for your frailty.

Sitting by the fire in the cozy cabin, looking out at the snow and fierce cold, I thought about the people who lived here before me, way before me. Before wood could be delivered for the stove, before electricity, before hot water and phones. How did they do it? I wouldn't have lasted an hour out there that day, and that's even allowing for my modern boots and coat. What was it like to live in this country when all you had to keep you warm was your furs and knitting? My stack of woollies was drying by the fire. My mittens, hat, leg warmers, sweater, scarf—all of that to fight the cold with, and I still would have been in very serious trouble right quick if I had made even a minor error.

I'm sure the people who lived here were smart and tried not to get into trouble. Some of them probably froze to death anyway. I like to think that those were the stupid people, but I also like to think I'm smart, and I very nearly could have ended it all out there because I misinterpreted the track of a deer. I'm sure that the Canadians before me got lost, fell down cracks, miscalculated the time, got caught in blizzards, and never found their way home in the snow. I can even imagine them, putting on all their knitted stuff to go to the barn, winding a long scarf around their faces while thinking, "Stupid cows. I hope I come back alive from this." In weather like this, in a place like this, for all my bravado and pride in being swathed in handknits to fight the cold, as sure as I am that I am better off than non-knitters in any battle against the winter, the truth is that without your brains, this place will have you. In weather like this, my knitting is simply a very minor insurance policy. My alpaca hat gives me maybe ten more minutes to get myself out of trouble. My wool socks, perhaps an extra fifteen before frostbite interferes with my ballet career (it could happen—don't dampen my dream). In this place, knowing how to knit might be something that buys me a little more time to figure my way out of a mistake, something that I think, as I cast on for another pair of mittens and look out at the snow, might qualify as being smart and not getting into trouble.

ODE TO A WASHER: A LOVE STORY IN THREE PARTS

PART ONE

From time to time, an appliance comes into the life of a human and finds its way into her heart. I know that seems unlikely, considering that in this love affair one being is animate and the other doesn't appear to be so, but such was the love between my washing machine and me. Intellectually I understand that he was an inanimate thing, but the truth is that my washing machine was there for me in a way that transcends all fact, and to me, he was a real and cherished personality in the house. That's why the day that my washer lay in the basement, disemboweled and de-hosed, ashamed, with his parts hanging out and some mysterious organ lying disassembled on the living room coffee table, in surgery, I felt real loss.

When I had moved into this house fourteen years earlier, it had a dryer but no washer. I was pretty sure (being thrilled just to have a house, never mind appliances) that I could live without a washing machine, which was good, because saying I was a little broke at the time would be like saying that teenagers are missing a little bit of common sense. I imagined myself loading up the play wagon with loads of laundry and three little girls and trouping off to the Laundromat. In the world of my imagination I had even convinced myself that this was better than having a washer, because where else other than the Laundromat can you do four loads of laundry at the same time? It was like having four washing machines, I told myself. This doomed arrangement lasted a mere ten days, until a stomach bug wracked the household one night and suddenly the idea of taking truly disgusting sheets and jammies down the street to the washer with sick kids hanging off of me like crabby accessories lost its romance faster than did Britney Spears's first marriage.

At exactly that fated moment, my sister had bought a new house, and it had a washing machine, but she owned a better one. The steady and deliberate appliance who would become my faithful Mr. Washie was dragged up out of her basement and then installed in mine by my brother and his buddy Pablo, whom I paid with a single case of mediocre beer.

It was instant love. From the moment that I first lifted his lid to the moment he fell ill, we had a happy and, at least for the first nine years of our association, entirely monogamous relationship.

(It's worth noting that it was I who wanted to open our love to other influences, not the honorable Mr. Washie.) In later years, this fine appliance had opened his heart to Joe and the girls and allowed them (even though they did not appreciate him the way that I did) to enter into a partnership of sorts. Through all of the loads of diapers, sheets, and dirty clothes, Mr. Washie never let me down. (There was that one time that I accidentally clogged his pump felting knitted clogs, but I bought him a new one and he forgave me for my carelessness.) Mr. Washie had done more to help me with this family than any other thing or person on Earth, with more reliability and quiet concern than my spouse and friends often showed, and I am not at all ashamed to admit that I loved him.

Mr. Washie and I had the sort of commitment that most married people only dream of, and although it was sort of accidental, I know some marriages that are the same. Five years ago Joe and I remodeled the kitchen, and, because we're not kitchen planners and are too cheap to hire one, we carelessly installed a large pantry near the basement door. That cupboard blocks the door to the basement a little bit, though not in a way you'd notice until you thought about putting appliances down there (or taking them out). There was no chance now of Mr. Washie ever coming out, or a new washer coming in without first removing a built-in pantry and its associated cupboards. That sort of built-in fidelity to each other meant that I was very committed to my relationship with Mr. Washie. I intended (because I sort of like the pantry too) that we would be staying together for the long haul, through thick and thin, sickness and health, so when Mr. Washie suffered a seizure one Friday, I implored Joe to go on a hunt for parts.

Joe, who is really rather handy, assessed the problem and figured which part needed a transplant. Then he called Sears (Mr. Washie's middle and last names are "Kenmore Heavy-Duty") and told them what washer we had. The lady on the other end of the phone asked for the model number printed on the back. Joe told her. Then she asked again. Joe told her again. She asked if there were any other numbers. Joe lay on the floor of the basement with a flashlight, and once again read the numbers to her with absolute precision.

"You're sure?" the Sears lady asked. Joe, in a supreme demonstration of willpower, did not point out to her that he can read numbers—all of them, 1 through 9—with remarkable accuracy. He simply said, "Yes. That's all it says." The woman went away then, and when she came back she said something shocking. She had found Mr. Washie's date of birth: 1978. My washing machine was a staggering twenty-eight years young.

Joe found this remarkable, and I was overwhelmed. This idea, that my noble and fierce washer was the appliance equivalent of a senior citizen, just about brought me to tears. I was suddenly so moved by his years of service to me that I could barely find the words for it. He had done easily 3,500 loads of laundry in this house, and there was no way to know what he had accomplished in the eighteen years he washed and spun before he came to live with me. I didn't even clean his filter as often as I should (which is something I felt really badly about after learning his handicap). He had been in at least two basement floods, but that dear machine still did two loads of jeans and a whack of towels before falling ill that Friday.

Joe kept talking to the lady, and it turned out that Sears still made the part Mr. Washie needed, that it was a mere $30, and that Joe knew how to put it in. This was more than my heart could take, and I vowed to clean the outside of the washer with an old soft diaper to show my gratitude, but it didn't feel like enough. Joe and I were so moved—me by my love of Mr. Washie, and Joe by the love of things that can be fixed in an hour for thirty bucks without disassembling a kitchen—that we had a little ceremony, there in the dingy basement, attended by cobwebs. We gave him a title. Let it be known far and wide across the land, that the noble washing machine formerly known as "Mr. Washie," in recognition for his many long years of service, his unfailing loyalty and decent felting, for withstanding basement floods and holding his lid high even though he had not been given so much as a wipe in a couple of months, for his dignity, class, and not needing us to call a repair person who would have taken us for a serious ride, was thereby dubbed Sir Washie. We attached a magnet that had a picture of the Stanley Cup to the front of him to make it official.

PART TWO

A few months later, right before Christmas, I was behind on everything—the shopping, the knitting, the housekeeping—and even though I'm perpetually behind on the laundry, I realized that we were about to hit critical mass. It was to the point where people were soon going to have to stay home because they didn't have clean underwear, and so I tossed a load into Sir Washie. Now, I've explained that Sir Washie was my dearest friend in the world. I freely admit I'd had some pretty warm feelings about a few sexy front loaders I'd seen, but that's like still loving your husband even though you think Pierce Brosnan is hot. Totally normal. In any case, I tossed a load in, came upstairs, and got on with my day. Later, when I went down to switch things over to the dryer (for which I hold no affection at all), I lifted his lid, reached into his innards, and discovered, with the sinking heart and feeling of impending doom that any laundry-slacking mother can identify with, that the clothes were all sopping wet. Soaked. It was like getting a phone call that your ninety-six-year-old aunt has had a stroke. You know she might be okay, but really, what are the odds that it isn't the beginning of the end? Sir Washie was full of wet clothes, but not water, so I was pretty sure that he had suffered some sort of episode that left him able to agitate and drain but had stripped him of his critical ability to spin.

I'm sure that I don't have to tell you that this was a full-blown crisis, and one for which I accepted all responsibility. I had noticed that Sir Washie was making an odd noise, but truthfully I didn't look into it because I thought it was just age—I mean, Joe makes all sorts of noises now that he didn't when he was a younger guy, and there's nothing really wrong with him. I should have known, after all of these years of appliance ownership, that washing machines just don't make odd noises. Washing machines make expensive noises, and I should have gotten him help right away. Instead, I looked the other way, and now, because I am not only the sort of woman who ignores an appliance in need, but also the sort of woman who doesn't wash anything until people have no pants or towels, I found myself completely screwed. I personally was screwed while wearing a dirty old T-shirt and pants with coffee spilled on one leg, but I work from home, where it doesn't matter if you're wearing strange clothes. This crisis was going to be harder to break to Joe and the kids, since they were going to have to leave the house each day wearing last Christmas's elf jammies. I looked at the budget and realized that unless that washer was fixable for about $1.46, somebody's Christmas present was going to have to be the gift of this family not smelling funny. That bummed me out for about six seconds, and then I thought about it, and considering how I felt about Sir Washie and his contribution to the family . . . I'd take it. Wrap up a fixed washer and stick a bow on it. I'd be thrilled.

Joe went downstairs with the flashlight and a screwdriver, and it was only about fifteen minutes before he was back upstairs. I could tell the news was not good. Standing there, in the kitchen, he told me that Sir Washie was sick enough to need professional help. Brokenhearted, I started calling around to find a repair guy, preferably one who wanted to be paid in sock yarn.

PART THREE

*I*t is with tremendous sadness that I write to tell you of the passing of my dear friend, helpmate, and tireless companion, Sir Washie. Sir Washie, a thirty-year-old Kenmore heavy-duty washer of extraordinary merit, departed this home yesterday after a short illness, which ended when the fourth repairman we called laughed himself into a coughing spasm rather than come out and even look at our appliance, saying that all he would do if he came to give us an estimate was charge us $100 for a death certificate. (Apparently he, like the other three repairmen, could tell from their cars that Sir Washie was suffering from a terminal illness, which I thought was rather unfair to my washer, and I told them so.)

I have relayed my deep love for Sir Washie and the many magical things he did for me. From his noble rendering of clean diapers when the girls were little, to the countless towels the teenagers foisted upon him in his old age, he selflessly served this family. He was patient, learning to enter into new relationships over the last few years as Joe and the girls sought (reluctantly) to share in the joy of coming to know him, and gently drawing their attention to the unbalanced loads they placed within him by politely thumping across the room. Even when they forgot to clean his lint filter he was understanding, and he never once spoke of the time that I clogged his pump felting six pairs of clogs for Christmas presents.

Perhaps his greatest gift to this family was that he never once, in all of the time that we were together, burdened us with a repair bill at a time when we couldn't manage it—even after having his bottom parts dipped in a fourteen-inch-deep icy basement flood, he just kept on washing. He was considerate that way. Sir Washie is the only entity on this Earth that helped me just about every day without complaining, judging, or expecting anything from me, and he will be sorely missed.

He will be especially missed because, as expected, his demise created a nightmare chain of events. Joe and I went shopping to replace him (and his slacker dryer friend, who is a limping piece of crap that I don't love at all) and we carefully chose the smallest appliances we could that were still full-sized and reasonably priced. (Did you know that there are $4,000 washing machines? Seriously. If a washer is $4,000 I want it to get the laundry out of my room and bring it back folded after it made me coffee and told me it likes my hair. $4,000. Boggles the mind.)

When the new washer arrived on New Year's Eve, the delivery guys went downstairs, fetched up dear Sir Washie as though he were common trash, hauled him up the basement steps, then were stopped by that pantry. I had been sure that this would be the case, but I still let them try. I thought maybe they knew a trick that would mean that I didn't have to trash my kitchen, but they didn't.

In our family, it is tradition to tidy up on New Year's Eve. In fact, I usually clean for a few days leading up, believing that how your affairs are when the New Year dawns is how your affairs will continue for the coming year. We end as we mean to go on, and the idea of trashing the house—really trashing it—on New Year's Eve hit my superstition button hard. What would it mean for the New Year if your kitchen was partly disassembled as the calendar hit the reset button? I'd tried to get the appliance delivered the day before just to avoid this, but here I was.

While the first seeds of hysteria were sown within me, my pantry was emptied, unscrewed, detached, and removed, and the gentle Sir Washie finally came through the kitchen, went out the back door, and was taken far away. I felt badly for him as I stood at the back door watching him disappear into the night. I wondered if he would be alright right before—well, right before I remembered he was an inanimate object that had no feelings and that it was really only me wracked by grief . . . but I was distracted from my grief process by a crisis that had begun to develop back in the kitchen.

The new washer is the same depth as Sir Washie but about four centimeters wider. This, we thought, was going to make it hard to get it downstairs, but not impossible. As I was still drying my tears, this was proving to be wrong. Even with the pantry removed (and lying in the hall) the new washer wouldn't even clear the doorway. Joe said it was just a small part of the door frame that was the problem, which was no problem, because he could "make it work." That little piece came off, another attempt was made to get the new washer in, and then Joe, with a zeal that was only matched by my sense of foreboding, announced that all we needed to do was remove a bigger piece of the door frame itself, and then we would be home free. He started to assemble his tools, and for some crazy reason probably related to insurance coverage, the minute he used the words "Sawzall," "pry bar," and "widen" the delivery guys panicked, got in their truck, and gunned it out of here.

Joe called in the forces. My brother Ian and our friend Ken came to help, and our neighbor Greg provided a variety of saws and emotional support. (He may also have been watching his back, since his house is the other half of our semidetached, and once Joe started talking about sawing anything at all near a shared wall, Greg was keenly interested.) I should have known how it was going to go down when my brother bolted through the front door with a big smile on his face and said "I'm here to help. I didn't miss all the sawing . . . did I?" That was when I had my first drink.

In a flurry of sawdust and optimism, the guys removed the facing board and tried again to lower the washer. Nope. They reconsidered and hacked another board out of the frame. Still not big enough. They sawed another part of the frame out and then removed a light switch (on the theory that every centimeter counted) and with chaos and saws all around them, this time the washer cleared the door. There was much jubilation, but it was short lived.

I had my second drink as they discovered that the washer (for whom I was beginning to feel a resentment nearly matched by my longing for the departed Sir Washie) would only go down the first two steps to the basement before the team encountered another problem in the form of the main sewer line on their left, and a wall on their right. Thankfully, nobody said anything about the sewer line, but it was decided very quickly that the wall couldn't entirely remain if the washer was going to go down. I looked at Joe talking about hacking up more of the house, and I didn't think he looked as worried as he should. In fact, he was standing in the basement with a large saw, a sweaty brow, and a crazy, determined look in his eye, all while smiling in a really strange way and saying, "I can do it, I can do it. I have momentum!"

At this point, I completely flipped out. I called a halt to operations while I stood in the kitchen and took stock for a minute. We had removed the door, the food, the cabinet, the door frame, and the light fixtures, and we had sawed off chunks of the house. The house was trashed. The kitchen was trashed. There was a new washer mocking me from the back door, and nobody had clean clothes. I could tell that doorway would never be right again and we were a few hours from the start of the New Year while my husband delightedly planned to take out a part of our house that was in his way.

I took a deep breath and gave a thoroughly impassioned speech about how we had crossed the crazy line. Totally crossed it. I told Joe that one of the things I love best about him is his optimism. He always believes that everything is going to work out, and I could see that Joe had decided that this washer was going into the basement no matter what it took. He was on a mission. I told him that I really loved his optimism, but that this time it just wasn't appropriate. This wasn't going well and I didn't think it was going to start going well and the washer was too damn big and I had changed my mind and we needed to absolutely return it right now before he sawed up anything else. We needed to return this washer and pay the extra money and get apartment-sized appliances. I had said I didn't want them because I'd have to do a load of laundry every fourteen minutes for the rest of my life but right that minute I didn't care because, frankly, I had hit my limit for a sawed-up house, and saws, and washers, and problems. I burst into tears, while the assembled masses looked at me like they couldn't understand how any of this could be bothering anyone.

That is when I saw it. There was a huge scratch on the side of the washer, and I realized that it couldn't be returned. That thing, that monstrosity that wouldn't fit down the stairs, would belong to us forever. As that dawned on me, I was suddenly filled with an urge to hack a hole in the floor of the kitchen and just drop the bastard through to the basement, or maybe shove it onto the stairs and leap upon it with the full force of my body until it fell through, smashing whatever needed to be smashed to make it work. I took a deep breath. I poured myself a third drink, and then I told them all to put down their tools and get out.

EPILOGUE: OR, THE REASONS WHY I AM TRYING TO LOVE MY NEW WASHING MACHINE*

5. It is in the basement, not the kitchen. The next day, when I had recovered sufficient will to go on, it turned out that only one small part of one old wall needed to come down, and then the washer descended to the basement with as little

difficulty as a four hundred pound washer can while being moved through a very, very narrow house by men who have been moving a washer for two days and aren't really excited about it anymore. Turns out that Joe's optimism was not only well placed, but necessary.

4. Not to sound ungrateful for the years of service Sir Washie gave me, but it would appear that there have been some improvements in washing machines in the last thirty years. (Who knew?) For example, the interior of this front loader is so big that not only will it hold every towel in the house, but I also think I could rent it out as an apartment if we're ever short of cash again. It holds so much stuff that if you bug your kids to do their laundry, and you finally manage to convince them to go and do it, they can do all of their laundry in one load and that means that you're only going to have to fight with them about laundry and how people really do care how they smell once every week, not twice. I will lay down my life for anything that makes for fewer fights with my kids.

3. It makes virtually no noise. I loved Sir Washie, but the sound of him running through a cycle was something that made you nervous no matter where you were in the house, and a slightly unbalanced load (like many of us in our last

months, Sir Washie was mostly unbalanced toward the end) could shake windows, scare small children, and be generally louder than a fifteen-year-old stripped of a cell phone on a Friday night just after she found out that the new boy who moved in next to her friend said that he thought her hair was "sorta nice."

2. For weeks, we had been taking our laundry over to my mother-in-law's. This means that you bundled up yourself and your laundry, walked over to her place in varying types of freezing precipitation and over a variety of forms of ice, washed the laundry, and walked back, freezing your arse all the way. This is a huge chunk out of one's workday, so we tried not to dirty clothes. Finally having a washer in the house meant that the next time someone spilled coffee, I could mop it up with a towel, rather than scream "Drink it off the floor! Drink it off the floor! Are you crazy! Don't touch that towel!" like I did three days earlier when the last clean towel in the house looked like it needed to be guarded with my life.

1. When Sir Washie finished a load (heaven bless him) he did nothing but lay there quietly, trying to recover from the effort. When the new washer finishes, it plays a song.** Joe thinks that the purpose of the song is to tell you that the

load is finished, but I don't think so. I think it plays a song because it's just so thrilled to be serenely fulfilling its highest purpose by doing my laundry. I think it's trying to tell me that there is nothing else in the world that would satisfy it more than churning away so we can have clean gitch. I think it's delighted to be in my service.

I think it's happy here, and I hope that Sir Washie knows that, song or no, I do still miss him.

---

*My love for my new washing machine should in no way be taken as a lack of loyalty to the memory of Sir Washie. He was the best washer ever and can never really be replaced no matter how seriously slick his replacement is.

**The song is "Die Forelle" ("The Trout") by Schubert. I am totally not kidding.

PERSONAL FILTERS

A while ago I was having coffee with an acquaintance, and when I pulled out my knitting to do a few rounds, she glanced around quickly to see who was looking, and then said, "Are you really going to do that in public?" I laughed, because it wasn't like I was picking my nose, shaving my armpits, or loudly telling sexually explicit jokes, and I struggled to figure out how knitting was even on the list of things that she would consider embarrassing to be caught at. I wanted to ask her what she was thinking, but I didn't know her very well and, truthfully, I was worried about the answer she might give me. Obviously in her world, being a knitter was embarrassing, and doing it meant something about you that you wouldn't want other people to know—what, I couldn't imagine. I thought of about a hundred snappy answers to her question while I was sitting there, answers like, "No, of course I'm not really going to do this in public. I just carry yarn with me as a prop so that I can repel people who are cool and hip like you," or even just, "Yes. I like myself and I don't worry much about what people think, especially if it has nothing at all to do with them." As always, none of them came out of my mouth, because I have excellent personal filters. I think that what I said instead was something like, "Oh sure. I'm already a slightly dumpy mother of three in my forties. I have nothing to lose".

All the way home from the coffee shop, I imagined a world where, when people say something stupid to me about knitting, I just say what I'm thinking. Just let go, roll with the adage that if you ask a stupid question, you should get a stupid answer, and let it rip. I know I'd never really do it, because it's wrong to make people feel bad, even if they deserve it, but still, when I got home I wrote a list. Even just getting it down on paper makes it more likely that I won't ever say it out loud.

THINGS THAT NON-KNITTERS SAY TO ME AND WHAT I WOULD LIKE TO SAY BACK
(but Never Will Because I am a Good Person)

SCENE: *Me, knitting. Non-knitter approaches and says, "Wow, are you knitting?"*

WHAT I WOULD LIKE TO SAY: Nope, doesn't it look like it though? Really, this is a careful illusion made possible through my many years of studying enchantment and magic. In reality, I'm just sitting around like everyone else, but I make it appear as though I'm knitting to create a feeling of coziness, make me look smart, and give me a way to meet people. Hi!

WHAT I ACTUALLY SAID: Yes.

SCENE: *Me, knitting on an airplane. Non-knitter looks at me and says, "Did they let you through security with those?"*

WHAT I WOULD LIKE TO SAY: No. Security did *not* allow me through with these knitting needles. Instead of coming through security just like everyone else on this plane, I had to come up with an extremely complicated plan. This morning, before I left home, I positioned the needles on my person and then when I passed through the X-ray machine I told them it was a steel plate I have from the war. When they looked suspicious and snapped their latex gloves, I ran. I bolted past the desk, deliberately abandoning my things in the search machine (having strategically removed all identifying materials ahead of time), and streaked through the airport, hiding briefly in a Starbucks to elude Homeland Security. When I saw them pass, I used the door codes I'd stolen from a pilot I shagged last week to open the gates, and slunk through the back corridors of the airport, stepping in every puddle I could find to avoid leaving a scent for the tracking dogs. I backtracked, made only left turns, and briefly rappelled until I made it all the way back to my original gate where I used a counterfeit German passport to sneak onto the plane. Now, I'm sitting here, knitting, and celebrating the fact that, even though I have certainly secured myself at least fifteen years in federal prison, if not a violent shooting death upon landing (assuming, of course, that I am not taken out by an Air Marshall long before arrival), I have at long last met my goal of sneaking needles past security so that I can at long last knit a damn sock on a plane! (At this point I imagine I would laugh maniacally.)

WHAT I ACTUALLY SAID: Yes.

SCENE: *Me, knitting and appearing to enjoy it. Non-knitter says, "You knit a lot. Do you enjoy it?"*

WHAT I WOULD LIKE TO SAY: No, I can't stand it. It's fiddly and dumb and the needles keep poking holes in my purse, but you know what? I bought hundreds of skeins of yarn before I was sure about it, and I'm no quitter. As soon as I get this yarn used up I'm off it. It was a horrible mistake.

WHAT I ACTUALLY SAID: Yes.

SCENE: *Me, knitting socks. Non-knitter approaches and asks what I'm making. I tell the person that it's socks, and we have a brief conversation about how long it takes to make a pair of socks, at which point the helpful non-knitter tries to release me from my slave labor by telling me something that I obviously don't know, or I wouldn't be knitting socks. The non-knitter asks, in all sincerity, "Did you know that you can get socks for a dollar a pair at Walmart?"*

WHAT I WOULD LIKE TO SAY: Are you serious! Really? Why didn't someone tell me this before now? I feel dizzy. I need to sit down. Do you know how much time it takes to make a pair of socks? Do you know how much time in my life I've spent on this? It takes forever to knit socks—and it's boring and expensive! Please, I beg of you! Take me to this mysterious and magical "Walmart" so that I too may have socks that don't need to be knit! Oh, happy, happy day! Now if only something could be done about sweaters.

WHAT I ACTUALLY SAID: Yes.

SCENE: *Me at my spinning wheel, making yarn. Non-knitter asks me what I am doing. I reply, "making yarn." Non-knitter asks, "Real yarn?"*

WHAT I WOULD LIKE TO SAY: No, not real yarn. Real yarn can only come from a machine and a store. Spinning wheels are a way of replicating yarn, but it's not usable, just ornamental. It actually disintegrates after a few hours and leaves only a pile of lint.

WHAT I ACTUALLY SAID: Yes.

SCENE: *Me, knitting away, no pattern in sight. Non-knitter approaches and asks where my pattern is. I reply that I'm not using one. She looks boggled for a moment, and then asks, "If you don't have a pattern, aren't you worried about what you'll end up making?"*

WHAT I WOULD LIKE TO SAY: I really am. I'm hoping it doesn't turn out to be another hat, because that's what it was the last two times I knit without a pattern. I like the element of surprise, though—the way that when I don't use a pattern, it's all up in the air. Could be a sweater, could be mittens, no way to know until I'm finished. It's fun, but frustrating.

WHAT I REALLY SAID: No.

SCENE: *I'm knitting, as I usually am, and I'm approached by a non-knitter who points out that every time she sees me, I'm knitting. "You knit a lot," she observes. What comes out of her mouth next is the only thing a non-knitter has ever said to me that has effectively silenced not just my actual voice but my inner one as well.*

"You must have a lot of time on your hands. You should think about getting a hobby."

OUT OF THE CLOSET

$\mathcal{I}$ live in a teeny-tiny house, one of several in a row, built more than 130 years ago for the workers of a nearby piano factory. (In an odd twist of fate I actually own one of those pianos, built by someone who lived in my house. I like that.) These are thrifty, odd little houses, and everything about them and even the street I live on tells a story about what things used to be like here. For example, nobody has a driveway (because nobody owned a car) and yet the street is twice as wide as all the others in the neighborhood because there used to be a dairy nearby and the horse-drawn milk wagons needed room to turn. My little house sits right at the sidewalk, with only a few square meters for a front garden, and over the years the whole house has increasingly begun to list toward the light post. (I'm almost afraid to look into that.) The history of this place and its odd little quirks give this house a set of charms that you won't find in a new house in a modern suburb, although I admit that I do occasionally (and by "occasionally" you understand that I mean "pretty often") envy those dwellers something. While I love my claw-foot tub,

I sometimes think about what it would be like to have water pipes big enough to grant sufficient water pressure for a shower, and while my friends in newer homes can plug something in without a thought, I live with electrical wiring that seems to have been installed by M. C. Escher and scares the living snot out of every electrician I hire to try and make sense of it. While it was charming, and even knitterly, to discover that parts of my home are insulated with newspaper and wool, in the February of the Canadian winter I consider nothing but the dead sexy nature of modern and efficient insulation. There is much that I have pined for, but if I had to drill it down to one thing I have always wanted, always wished that this little house had, it's something I bet you never thought about taking for granted. It's closets.

Oh, as the mother of three daughters, how I have longed for closets. At the turn of the century, when this house was built, closets weren't at all in vogue. People owned very few clothes and when they did hang them up, it was on hooks, not hangers, so closets were hardly an efficient use of space. As a result, the closets in Victorian homes are often sparse, and tiny, and without a rod to hang hangers on. If you do install a rod in your tiny little closet, the closet itself is hardly deep enough to accommodate hangers—many of us end up choosing between having hangers and having doors on our closets. My entire house has (brace yourself) two closets. Two. Two tiny closets so small that one of those plastic storage bins—the ones that are about two and a half feet long, and about one and a half feet deep—barely fits. That's small. There is no coat closet (we have hooks by the door), no linen closet (we have a wardrobe for towels and sheets), and most importantly, and I'm sure you can feel me here, nowhere to shove the mess if someone is coming over and you really need to hide all the dirty laundry. There is no closet big enough to be a proper hide-and-seek spot, and the phrase "come out of the closet" held no meaning for my children until they were old enough to grasp it as a metaphor, because if you told them someone should come out of the closet they would stare blankly at you wondering why, or actually *how*, whoever it was got in there.

Now all of this, this closet talk, is important here, not just because closets are great places to keep yarn—I've developed all kinds of entirely radical and innovative yarn storage skills as a result of my closet shortage—but because of what that means. No closets means that the yarn habit can't be in the closet, and so the people who live here have to get down with my yarn situation pretty quickly, because it is impossible to live in a closetless house with a knitter and have the yarn be a secret. It just doesn't work, and that extends to all of your belongings, no matter what you tend to hoard. Having no closets breeds a certain sort of openness and honesty about your stuff and how much of it you have. If you can't hide things, if you can't just decide not to decide if you have to have them and stick them in a tiny room with a door and no light created in your home just for the purpose of holding things, then you have to start deciding about what you're going to keep and what you're not. If space is at a premium—and you don't know at what sort of a premium closet space is until you've lived with three teenage girls, a knitter, and a man who has kept (he's very sentimental) every item he's ever owned—and you have only two closets, then you have to make crazy, harsh, and deliberate decisions about two things. You need to know what—in a culture that says you should have more and new stuff all the time—is exactly worth having, and you need to embrace the idea of sharing that space and negotiating what is important to each of those five people, given that all of you will be competing with Olympic vigor for said limited space.

Over the years that we've lived like this, it's the last point that we've struggled with the most. Sure, it's hard to prune our belongings down to reasonable levels and to fight the wave of consumerism that tells us we should have a lot more stuff than what fits in those closets, but it is the ranking system that gives all of us the most grief. When the girls were little it was easier. Homes with little children are more dictatorships than democracies, and it was up to me to decide what the girls owned, how much of it got kept, and what was important. Extensive Barbie stashes were kept reined in by periodic nocturnal abductions, and from time to time a kid looked at us suspiciously when a vast collection of rocks from a neighborhood park simply vanished while they were out. But by far and away, the dictators dictated what stayed and what didn't, and the closet space was shared the way we thought it should be. As the girls have grown older, this has gotten more challenging. For starters, they sleep less, giving me far less opportunity to rifle a closet and collect things that I don't approve of, and it's been my experience that they have way stronger feelings about waking up to discover you squatting on the floor in the dark, tossing out half their collection of outgrown T-shirts into a bag for charity. (For the life of me, I cannot understand why you would have an emotional attachment to an outgrown, plain T-shirt that has to drive your mother to abscond with it in the night. It's not like it's from a U2 tour in the '80s, which is my husband's excuse for his.)

Now that my daughters are young women, I have come to realize that I need to make my closet points with logic and common sense. A box of books that you don't love enough to have on a shelf for re-reading? Sell or donate. You won't forget what you've read, and if you won't re-read it, it has no purpose here. Clothing that you will never, ever wear again? Sell or donate. Toys that aren't fun anymore? Out. The charger for a cell phone that you had four years ago that got lost but might come in handy if you ever find the phone? (Which, I'd like to point out, is super unlikely if your room is always a sty like that . . . but I digress.) Gone. Twelve green T-shirts? No duplicating. Pare it down. Seven binders from grade eight French? Nobody's testing you on that again. Moving on. The skanky tank top I don't want you to wear at home, never mind in public, and I keep stuffing behind the board games so you can't find it? Give it up. Bottom line rule: If an item is not going to be used by us, then it doesn't get to use our space.

Gradually, as the girls have grown old enough to be included in our ranking system, and to be respected (mostly) for their personal choices and what they would like to keep, they have also grown old enough to challenge the things that my husband and I have in those closets. While I thought this was pretty fun when they were suggesting that Joe didn't really need a box of sailing magazines from the summer he was sixteen (I have long believed the same, and was thrilled that they had grown into young women of such common sense), the rollicking good time that is judging the choices your mate makes and holding them accountable for it stopped being all that much fun when that same keen eye was turned toward the stash. When a family is gathered in front of a closet, jockeying for enough room for a snowboard and two pairs of inline skates (that no one ever uses, that's all I'm saying) everybody's stuff is suspected of being useless and taking up valuable space. The next thing I knew, we had finally and entirely moved from a dictatorship to a democracy, and my kids were asking me to justify the yarn-based use of a closet.

The ladies had several arguments and were so well organized that they resembled the debate equivalent of a yarn stash black ops strike force. If clothes they will not be wearing had to go, they suggested, then why not yarn I will not knit? Some of that yarn, they argued, has been in that closet since we moved here. In a stunning example of turning my own logic against me, they suggested that if I had not used it in ten years, then I maybe wasn't going to. Wasn't that what I said to Meg about the bead making kit she's been saving since her eighth birthday, just in case there's some sort of crazed emergency that demands handmade beads? Besides, Sam proffered strategically, hadn't I told her that saving an extra radio was ridiculous, since there was little chance that she would need it, and it could be easily replaced if there was a need? Didn't that, she cannily noted, apply to merino? From there, things went downhill, as Joe spotted the opportunity for a little sport.

"We don't store duplicates," Joe said, "and thirty skeins of sock yarn are all sock yarn. That's duplicating." His eyes practically twinkled. "If I can't have five caulking guns, then you can't have thirty skeins of sock yarn." Now he was playing with me. He knew damn well that there was a snowflake's chance in hell that even one of the skeins was leaving; he was just enjoying watching me justify it. All I could think was "Keep laughing, buddy, because the 'resistor collection' that you're saving 'just in case' and is practically all duplicates is next, and I'm going after the five amplifiers after that."

"He's right," said Megan, but she didn't seem very sporting.

"This closet is family space, and the other day when you were in here, you said that you couldn't imagine what you were thinking when you bought those five skeins of linen. If that's true, then shouldn't they be sold or donated?"

The kid had a point. They all had a point, but the longer I stood there, the more convinced I became that I wasn't wrong. How would I explain to them how the stash was different? That their things didn't deserve to be here, but mine did? How did I find a place where taking this much space for my stuff was more worthy and valid than whatever stuff they were attached to? They were right about a few things. I do have a lot of yarn. That much I can't argue. A lot of that yarn might never get knit, and if I got rid of the yarn, I could always get more—easily, even. I stood there and tried to come up with my justification. I thought about telling them that knitting is not just my stuff; it's me. I thought about telling them that none of it was really replaceable. I thought about telling them this: That the stash was not just stuff taking up our meager closet (and shelf) space. The beauty and the necessity of it all was that every skein of it was pure potential and inspiration. Where Sam certainly wasn't going to use the outgrown T-shirts (and I certainly wasn't going to let her use the skanky one), I might use the stash. Maybe, and that "maybe" made all the difference. I could haul off and knit all that sock yarn, every skein of it, and they aren't duplicates. They're all different and unique and most of them are handpaints and that, my friends, that fact makes them unique all by itself. They're art, and they haven't even been knit yet. Do people ask you why you have art in your house, even though it's unnecessary? Do people question painting your walls a color, even though having white walls serves the same purpose? Did people ask Renoir why he was keeping all those canvases around? No sirree, they did not, and if his family had gotten all uppity about the paint in the closet, he would have told them all that there were lots of paintings inside those paints, and that all he did was release them, and therefore it stands to reason that he needs all those paints and canvases because the art couldn't exist otherwise. Well, that's how I feel about the sock yarn. All those skeins are larval sock art, and while we're at it, this family is standing here in front of the closet all looking pretty damn smug, going after the stash that put those cozy handknit socks right on their feet. Do you—I thought about saying—do you wanna slap a pair of crappy store-bought socks on your feet before you challenge me on this, you bunch of ingrates?

Those are all things that I thought about saying, but in the end I went another way. I stood up, wiped any look of shame off of my face, plunked down my box of yarn in its rightful space, turned to face my kids, and said the most important thing.

I own the closet. You're screwed.

A LITTLE DEMORALIZING

$\mathcal{A}$ bout 12:30 one night, as I sat trying to make knitting headway on a little sweater and waiting for Joe to come home, the phone rang. I answered, since a phone call at 12:30 a.m. usually means something very interesting is happening, and lo, it surely was.

Me: "Hello?"
Joe: "You're not going to believe this."

Now, it was a week before Christmas, the washer was broken, we were under the gun to get Christmas ready, I was on a "knitting schedule," the news was calling the snowstorms headed our way "Snow-maggedon," and we had just found out that neither of us was getting paid before the end of the year. There was not much that I wouldn't believe at that point, and Joe knew that, so "You're not going to believe this" was a pretty bold statement.

Me: "Okay. Go."

Joe: "I've got the pickup stuck at my Mum and Dad's and I can't get it out."

Me: "Really?"

Now, see that? He was right. Joe's from Newfoundland. He can drive in any amount of snow. Joe never gets stuck. Ever. Dude knows how to drive in any amount of stuff, and he's experienced enough to not drive if it's really not possible. If Joe was actually stuck, then I was stunned. I was also knitting, and it was after midnight and cold, so I was also really not buying that he needed me to get him out. If Joe couldn't handle a driving problem, I really wasn't going to be able to.

Me: "Seriously?"

Joe: "Seriously. Baby, I'm stuck."

Me: "Why don't you try a little longer, and if it turns out you're really stuck, then I'll walk over."

I said that because, frankly . . . I just could not believe Joe was stuck. I believed that what Joe was actually saying to me could be translated more like, "Honey, I'm frustrated so I wanted to share, but I'll work it out like I always do because, well, I'm Joe." I mumbled something sort of sympathetic, like, "I'm sure you'll get it" and hung up the phone and finished my row. About twenty minutes later the phone rang again, and I was pretty sure it was Joe calling to tell me that he was out, and I should never mind, and he'd be home in a minute.

Me: "Hello?"

Joe: "Baby, you gotta come help me. I'm really stuck. I'm so stuck. This is bad."

Bad? Joe doesn't get into bad trouble backing out of a parking spot at his mum's. It wasn't like she lives in rural Ontario and he could be in a ditch. It wasn't like there was a ten-foot snowdrift to be stuck in, or he had the car hanging off a cliff over the sea. He was three minutes from home in a back alley drive. Bad?

Me: "Bad?"

Joe: "You gotta come."

Me: "Joe, what's going on?"

Joe: "Well, I was trying to back out, but there was a BMW, so I didn't want to hit it, you know? So I pulled up between the garage and the light pole, but the truck slipped on the snow and ice."

Me: "Slipped? Why don't you get out and dig yourself out? Why don't you give up and we'll deal with it in the morning?"

Joe: "I told you, Steph. It's really bad."

We kept talking, and here's what I came to understand.

Joe had the pickup truck (which is a completely eccentric piece of junk that only starts every day due to a small miracle) parked at the bottom of his parents' garage. There was a BMW (which we can't afford to breathe on, never mind hit) parked behind him, so he pulled forward slightly, between the light pole and the garage, and was then going to reverse out. Unfortunately for Joe, as he drove forward, a most unexpected thing happened. The light rear end of the truck suddenly fishtailed out, the front end swung in (what with them being attached like they are), and whammo . . . The truck was suddenly and entirely wedged in diagonally between the garage and the light pole, which are, in a remarkable coincidence, spaced exactly as far apart as the truck is wide. Joe pulled forward, spun on the ice, tried to rock back, spun on the ice, and somehow, in a trick that reminds me of that crazy Chinese finger trap, only succeeded, with every minuscule move he was able to make, in wedging the truck ever more deeply between the garage and pole.

Every inch he convinced the truck to make smashed the sides of the truck in a little more, and by the time he called me, he was not only entirely and hopelessly stuck, he had smashed up the truck real good and had reconciled himself to the fact that any solution at all was going to involve ripping the mirrors off and further demolishing the sides of the thing. (Which, it turns out, he preferred to wrecking the side of his parents' garage, because even at forty years of age, wrecking your dad's stuff is A Big Deal.)

He couldn't ask his parents for help because he felt strongly that it would be best if they didn't see this, for the sake of the parent/child relationship and because he had only recently convinced them that he was the sort of adult who would never be in this fix. To ice the cake, and just to make sure that this event reached catastrophic proportions, the truck, jammed diagonally as it was, had the entire alley blocked so that nobody in the whole neighborhood could get their cars in or out when daytime came and they all tried to go to work or school. He was right. I didn't believe it, and It Was Bad.

Me: "Dude."

Joe: "Exactly. You gotta come over here."

Me: "Okay. Walk over and get me and we'll go back together. I'll try to rock it and you can push it."

Joe said nothing. The silence was deafening. Joe is the sort of man who would never have me walk a neighborhood alone in the night, and I couldn't figure out why he wasn't already on his way. Was he too frustrated? Was he too upset?

Me: "Honey?"

Joe said nothing. I heard him sigh.

Me: "Honey?"
Joe: "Steph. You don't understand."
Me: "Sure I do. Truck stuck. Very Bad. What aren't you
    telling me?"
Joe: "Steph. Think about it."
Me: " . . . ."
Joe: "Steph. The truck is wedged between the pole and the
    garage."
Me: "Got it."
Joe: "I don't think you do."

I waited and tried to figure it out. Obviously I was missing something, but I couldn't think what it was. Joe gave me a few minutes, and then he said it.

Joe: "Honey . . . The truck is stuck between the garage and
    the pole. I can't come get you. I can't open the doors."

This finished me. Entirely. I'd managed to hold it together until then, but that did it. The man had somehow gotten his truck wedged in an impossible situation, and not only had things gone from bad to worse, minute by minute, but that whole time, for the hour that he'd been trying to find a way out of it, he had been trapped in the truck and avoided telling me.

I collapsed on the floor, practically laughing myself sick. I kept laughing as I pulled on my boots, coat, and mittens. I kept laughing as I jogged the five minutes over to his parents'. I'd almost got a hold of myself as I rounded the corner to the alley, but dissolved helplessly again when I saw him. Truck wedged, sides deeply lacerated, mirrors askew, deep holes dug into the dirt and snow beneath it, with my husband sitting patiently, trapped in the dark. (For some reason, he wasn't laughing much.)

I shoved the truck hard while he rocked it, and somehow we managed to get it out of the rut it had dug so he could finally back up, scraping what was left of the paint off as we went. (We did not hit the BMW.) I came around and joined him in the truck, and we began to drive silently home. As we rounded the corner and he slowed the pickup, it shuddered a little and made a new noise, another variation on an automotive death rattle, sort of a "urrrrhhhhgggg," and it lurched around a bit. I looked at Joe. He looked ahead. We drove. At the stop sign we slowed again, and the truck repeated its mechanical-sea-cow-with-indigestion noise, and this time I asked Joe when that started. "At the thirty minutes stuck mark," he replied, and we drove on.

We got home, parked, and walked together quietly toward the house, and I was thinking about his ordeal. Any other person, I thought, would have expressed some sort of hostility or loud frustration by then, but Joe's a good-natured rock. If it had been me, trapped like that, trashing a truck in the dead of night, obstructing traffic, and listening to the transmission try to vomit itself out of the hood, you would have found me crazed in the thing, thrashing around screaming in a way that would have shamed the snot out of my mother—and she can compete at the Olympic level in obscenity, should the occasion demand it. I thought about that, and the bruises both the pickup and I would bear from my fists smashing against the interior in rage had that happened to me, and I looked at Joe. "You okay?" I asked him, trying to broach the idea that if he had a little anger to share I would listen, and he looked at me. He pulled off his boots. He smiled a bit, and he said:

"Honey. That was a little demoralizing."

I love that man.

DEATH NOTICE

*C*abled Grey (nee Skein)—A mostly finished sweater and long-time yarn resident of Stephanie's Stash in Toronto.

Cabled Grey died suddenly at home following a lengthy illness, surrounded by other knitting projects and a few knitters, on the 14th of November 2009. Cabled Grey was an ill-fitting sweater with raglan sleeves and largish cables, who began life as nine skeins of a pretty decent three-ply merino purchased at 20 percent off, and had marinated in the stash for about eight years. In his very early days, Cabled displayed a great deal of potential when executed as a beautiful gauge swatch, holding his shape and stitch definition, even when he was washed. Cabled will be remembered always for the promise he demonstrated when first wound into a ball of yarn, moments before his unfortunate infection with the terminal sweater pattern which was his eventual undoing. The yarns with whom he shared the work-in-progress basket fondly recall the cheerful way he endured re-knits due to errors in his chart, which of course became errors on his front, and for the way that he mostly managed to be a garment despite the way his raglan shapings were hopelessly miswritten in the pattern. They respected the way that Cabled held his ribbings high, despite the inescapable truth that there was absolutely no way that his designer had possibly written down the right number of stitches to pick up for his buttonband, leaving him eternally crooked round the front and neck.

In most obituaries, this is the part where one would say that the dearly departed fought valiantly or bravely, but such was not the case with Cabled Grey, who gave up on being a sweater faster than a sixteen-year-old can spend $50 at the mall. From the very moment that Cabled's back was cast on, he was tragically doomed, for even though his gauge swatch had twenty-eight stitches to four inches, it turned out that Cabled actually harbored a secret desire to have twenty-two stitches to four inches, which is a destiny that he manifested about midway through the second front, creating a sweater that had cardigan fronts of two dramatically different sizes, which would have been fine were the breasts of the recipient likewise as different as a tangerine and a watermelon, which they were not.

Cabled was ripped back several times in his life, but it never seemed to bother him at all, and, in fact, his knitter rather suspected that he was trying to prolong the knitting process by embracing the errors and re-knits. He was the sort of project that was really able to cut loose and let things happen. Even as his knitter was begging him to please get his gauge together and honor the commitment that is making a sweater, Cabled was able to stay true to his inner nature, which was that of a mercurial, flighty yarn with no real goals. (Suggestions that Cabled Grey may have had some hemp in his fiber content are untrue, but we see why knitters might have gotten the idea.) In fact it was the way that Cabled was happy just to be knit, not to be knit with any degree of quality, and his stunning ability to avoid becoming a sweater through passive aggressive behavior that earned him the playful nickname "total piece of crap."

Despite several interventions, treatments, re-knits, and pattern adjustments, Cabled Grey eventually succumbed to the terrible pattern he had contracted. One desperate final surgery was attempted, but the craftspeople present during this ill-fated procedure all supported the diagnosis of the original knitter, which was that Cabled should be helped to the great big cedar chest in the sky, and never attempted again. Cabled entered palliative care in the hall closet, until the 14th of November, when he received his final visit from neighborhood knitters during a "stash tidy." Knitters at the visitation were welcome to spend a few final moments with Grey, and every single one agreed wholeheartedly that it truly was best that this struggle end, as the knitter looked sort of desperate and frantic when Grey was taken from the bag, and it was clear that Cabled had an inoperable series of obviously miscrossed cables that were causing both him and his knitter a great deal of intractable pain.

Knitters surrounded Cabled at this time, and disconnected him from knit-support as they withdrew the needles. Shortly thereafter Cabled Grey came to the end of his repeat, and the knitters departed, sadly acknowledging that he was indeed hopelessly ugly and unfortunately ill-fitting, and had a really, really bad pattern. Services, as brief as they were, consisted of dumping the sweater into the Goodwill bin, while quaffing red wine and declaring "Life's too short for bad knits," "Don't let the door hit your arse on the way out," and the profound, "Holy cow, I can't believe I spent that much time and money on that sweater; man, I'm just pissed."

Cabled Grey, or rather the idea of what Cabled Grey could have been, will be sadly missed by his knitter, the needles he so persistently occupied, and the pattern that was his ultimate undoing. Cabled Grey is survived by his daughter, Leftover Grey Yarn, who is thinking about becoming a hat to honor her father. Blue Mohair, who occupied the space next to Cabled Grey on the shelf for many years, will miss him tremendously, although seems rather fond of the cute hand-dyed laceweight who's moved in. As usual, the sock yarns have no idea what is going on.

The departure of Cabled Grey was immediately followed by the casting on of Alpaca Lace Shawl, who shall be knit in his memory. In lieu of flowers, patterns without errors and yarn with good attitude may be sent to Stephanie's Stash, although truthfully, she's pretty much over it.

KNIT JUNKIE

We walk down the street together, my family and I, three blocks through the busy city from our front door to a little restaurant that we love, and as I take my seat and shrug off my cardigan, I reach down to my bag sitting by my feet. My hand goes in, and as it does there is more air in that bag than I expect, and my heart skips a beat. No knitting? I pull up the bag to my lap and open it, trying to understand what is going on. No knitting? I never have no knitting. I don't leave the house without knitting like other women don't leave the house without lipstick or a bra—neither of which I am wearing, but that's not the point. I always have knitting. It's one of the things I take with me each and every time I leave the house. Wallet, keys, phone, and a sock-in-progress. Hell, I usually have two kinds of knitting with me if I go to the kitchen, never mind a restaurant. I start pulling out things from my bag. No knitting. I look on the floor. Did I drop it? Maybe it's still with me? No knitting. That's it. I have no knitting with me. I pick up the menu and try to focus, but I am instantly and completely uncomfortable. I'm a creature of habit and my habit is more or less continuous knitting, and that's been true for decades, and now here I am in this restaurant and I don't have anything to knit and the waitress hasn't even taken our drink order yet, and this restaurant is good, but slow, and that means it's going to be a long time with no knitting and . . . I check my bag again to make sure that I didn't miss my knitting in there. Maybe it's under the gum. I rifle my belongings again, trying really hard to quiet the stirring panic.

Amanda, my eldest daughter, notices that I'm looking for something, probably because of the blizzard of receipts, stitch markers, notepads, and knitting patterns emerging from my bag and piling on the table in front of me, while I continue hopelessly looking for the yarn and needles I know now are sitting uselessly on the kitchen counter. "What are you looking for?" she asks, while I stare at the bottom of my bag, sweeping my hand across the surface like maybe my knitting has become invisible and that's why I can't find it. I see her brow crease with concern, and I realize that she can see I'm missing something important—something like a credit card or my wallet—and I can see that I'm about to be very poorly understood. I'm about to open my mouth to say that I forgot my knitting, and then there will be an eye roll of epic proportions, probably coupled with laughter around the table. I've been down this road before. I'm just about the only person in my house who would put the word "important" in front of the word "yarn," and I know what it looks like when I do. They aren't going to understand this. My love of yarn is unique in my family. I accept it, but I still try to avoid them looking at me like I'm a few elves short of an effective workshop, so when Amanda asks me what I'm missing, I just shove everything back into my bag, set it back at my feet, and smile. "Nothing, dear. It's okay. Have you looked at the menu?"

She hasn't, and as the minutes tick by, I start to figure out what I'll do. I'm looking at the menu but I'm not choosing what to eat. My thoughts keep getting dragged back to the knitting. We're three blocks from home. The walk here took about six minutes, and I think if I went to get my knitting I'd be back pretty quickly. I look around at my family and realize that again, this is going to be poorly understood, and I start tossing around the idea of sneaking out to get my knitting. I could excuse myself to go to the washroom, and then bolt off down the street at a dead run, collect the knitting, and tear back. If I really hustled I think I could do it in about seven minutes. Can I be missing for seven minutes?

I'm staring out the window plotting my route and feeling twitchy, when Joe asks me what's on my mind. I say it's nothing again, because I'm still trying to avoid looking crazy, and besides, I don't want to tip him off if I decide to go with the running thing. My youngest daughter, Samantha, who's always been the sort to notice things, has figured it out, though, and she spills the beans. "Mum forgot her knitting," she drawls, and I can tell that she's relishing the moment. "That's what it is. Mum forgot her knitting, and now she's twitching and thinking about going to get it. She can't get through a dinner without her knitting. She's not going to make it." Sam pauses here for effect, and I feel the urge to defend myself, but really I've been sitting there thinking the same thing. I did forget my knitting. I am freaking out. I am thinking about it and wondering what I'm supposed to do for the twenty minutes in between ordering and when the food arrives. The kid has a point. Sam peers at me over her menu and smirks. "You're addicted," she says. "You're a knitting junkie."

The family erupts into laughter, and they all begin to share stories about me for which my knitting friends would absolutely come to my defense. The time Mum couldn't knit because her finger was hurt, and she cleaned the whole bathroom with a toothbrush. The time that Mum ran out of yarn mid-hat and tried to make it to the store before it closed and fell down running. Running. For yarn. They whoop and roar, and while they do I'm thinking three things. First, none of these people are getting handknit bloody anything for Christmas. Second, that I really, really wish I had my knitting, because it's usually what keeps me from saying things I might regret later. Finally—and I guess this is the most important point—can knitting really be addictive? Am I a yarn junkie?

I make it through the dinner without going to get my knitting. It was clear to me that everyone thought that to sprint out the door, run three blocks to our house, grab my little sock off of the counter, and run back would be crazy. I read the look on their faces and could see that's what they thought. I even could see that there was nobody else knitting in the restaurant, so obviously it was both normal and possible to get through a meal without knitting, but that's not how it felt. I squirmed. I fidgeted. I thought about my knitting and how to get it the whole time. I was distracted and worried, and I wasn't just worried about how to get through a meal without my knitting; I was worried about other possibilities. What if, for example, on the way home there's a traffic jam or some kind of obstruction? Something that hauls us up or means we have to wait in the street. What if when we get back to our house, there's been a gas leak in the neighborhood and we can't go inside our house? What if we have to spend seven hours sitting on the curb waiting to be allowed back in? I can't do seven hours of waiting without knitting. I'll start to bother people or eat rocks or . . . As I sit there slightly sweaty, and definitely out of sorts, I wonder again.

Is this addiction? Can knitting truly be addictive? Are we all hooked on yarn and strung out on circulars? Couldn't stop if we wanted too? I've never met anyone who has told me that they are a recovering knitter, fresh out of twelve weeks of rehab, having almost lost their families, jobs, or happiness due to an unhealthy relationship with merino that they couldn't control; I do know lots of knitters who would be happy to tell you that they're uncomfortable and unhappy when they can't have their knitting. I know, too, that it's not like knitting is a hallucinogen or a straight-up psychoactive drug, but I tell you this: Knitting and yarn are absolutely mood-altering substances, and if you don't say so, you're lying. We wouldn't do it if it didn't have an effect. Some days, ten minutes with my knitting can save the lives of the humans who surround me, and it gives me the ability to cope with things I find difficult, such as waiting, or listening to people talk about shopping for pants. (It occurs to me that the last argument I'm making there is the same argument I once heard someone give as the reason it took two liters of wine a day to get through life, but let's set that aside for the moment.)

When I get home (no gas leak—my knitting and I are quickly reunited) I make some notes, and the next morning finds me at the reference library, looking for the *Diagnostic and Statistical Manual of Mental Disorders**, or DSM-IV, which is the American Psychiatric Association's book that defines all sorts of mental illness and disorders. I flip through the pages looking for addiction, substance abuse, dependency, all the keywords.I find out that "substance dependence" (which seems about right

*American Psychiatric Association, *Diagnostic and Statistical Manual of Mental Disorders*, 4th ed. (Washington, DC: American Psychiatric Association, 2000) 197-198.

for someone who wigged when she couldn't get her yarn) is defined as an individual showing any three or more specific criteria within a year. I slump down in the stacks, book wide open, and start to read the list.

(1) Tolerance, as defined by either of the following:
   (a) A need for markedly increased amounts of the substance to achieve intoxication or desired effect.
   (b) Markedly diminished effect with continued use of the same amount of the substance.

"Uh-oh" is my first thought. I reread the sentence, substituting "knitting" and "yarn" for "the substance." A need for markedly increased amounts of yarn? A diminished effect with the same amount of knitting? The sparks of concern are lit within me. If this were a quiz, most knitters I know would have to tick off that box. How much more yarn do I have now than I used to? How much more complex does the knitting have to be before it turns my crank? Admittedly I do still "use" garter and stockinette stitch, but ten years ago I didn't need a hit of lace to get through the weekend. Not a good sign—not to mention the fact that I'm more tolerant of what it costs. Used to be that if a skein of yarn was $20 I thought it was ridiculous. Now I'm all like "$20? What's the yardage?" I sigh. That's one.

(2) Withdrawal, as defined by either of the following:
- (a) The characteristic withdrawal syndrome for the substance.
- (b) The same (or a closely related) substance is taken to relieve or avoid withdrawal symptoms.

At first glance, I think I might get away on this one. It's not like knitters coming off of the good stuff get the shakes or are at risk of a seizure. We're just sort of antsy, obnoxious, weird, and fidgety, which, truth be told, isn't really withdrawal. At least in my case, it's the actual personality that I have without knitting. I knit because I'm not patient, because I can't wait well, because I'm fidgety, and it's not like that's characteristic. Most knitters who aren't knitting are just themselves, no matter who that is, for better or for worse; all different, just bored. I'm about to move on to the next criterion when I realize that it says "either" (a) or (b) could apply, and I realize that I'm hosed. Almost all knitters I know are going to substitute a closely related substance if they can't get what they usually use. If I couldn't get wool, I would use acrylic before I quit, and the two times in my life that I've had an injury that kept me from knitting? I broke out the crochet hook, and I don't even really like to crochet. Reluctantly, I mentally tick off this box too.

(3) **The substance is often taken in larger amounts or over a longer period than was intended.**

I only have one thing to say to that. Shut up. I always meant to have this much yarn, and for the record, I was planning the whole time to stay up that late knitting, and "just one more row" is simply a turn of phrase. Also, everybody has this many projects at once, and yarn in the freezer is normal. It keeps it safe from moths. Pass me my sock and get off my back.

(4) **There is a persistent desire or unsuccessful efforts to cut down or control substance use.**

Thankfully, I don't have to tick this box. Sure, I've de-stashed when things got a little wild, and there are times when the yarn budget has to be reined in, but that's just life, not addiction. It's not like I'm walking around saying, "Man, the hangover from last night's scarf is killing me. I can't tie one on with mittens tonight; I've got to cut back." Well, at least it's not like I'm saying it *that* much. (There have been a few incidents around the holidays, but everyone tends to overindulge then.) The same is true of yarn diets. There have been times when I'm choking the wool money, but that's the same as not buying much of anything when you're broke, and that's always successful. I've never told my kids that we're eating a single can of discount peas for dinner because Mummy blew the budget on merino, and what's more, I can honestly say that I have no desire—absolutely none—to cut back or control my knitting. As a matter of fact, I'd say I've got a persistent desire and I've made continuously unsuccessful efforts to increase my knitting and yarn use. I'm sure that these addiction book-writing people would just say something about needing to admit I have a problem, but screw it. I'm still going to work and cooking for my family; nobody who lives in my house is sharing a bed with a sibling because their room is full of yarn; and I say there's no problem to admit to.

(5) **A great deal of time is spent in activities to obtain the substance (e.g. visiting multiple doctors or driving long distances), use the substance (e.g. chain-smoking), or recover from its effects.**

As much as I was developing a righteous head of steam on that last one, number five is a problem. There are three yarn shops in town where they know me on sight, and at one of them I've lobbied to have a cubby to keep my things in, given how much time I'm there. I'd say that counts as spending a lot of time obtaining the substance, and we haven't even talked about how I go to knitting retreats, run knitting conferences, write and teach about knitting, and have, on more than one occasion, driven across many hundreds of miles to go to a sheep and wool festival for no other purpose than to "obtain the substance." Is that wrong? Is that addiction, or am I just really interested? I wonder, as I stare at the criteria on the page, what it means that every knitter I know spends tons of time obtaining the substance, and still tries to obtain more when they already have more than they can use. I try to relate it to an addict wandering the street looking for just a little to take the edge off, and realize that we're a different beast—sort of. A junkie is all about getting and using, and when that's used you need to get more. A knitter is all about getting and using, but not necessarily in that order, and there's a certain pleasure in having the substance with you without using it that (and I'm only guessing here) doesn't really seem to be the way it works with cocaine. With that thought, I resist the urge to check the DSM index for the criteria for hoarding, and move on.

(6) Important social, occupational, or recreational activities are given up or reduced because of substance use.

At first I think this one's okay too. For the most part, I haven't given up or reduced going to work or play because of knitting. As a matter of fact, it looks to me like my substance use increases my important social, occupational, and recreational activities. I go to a regular Knit Night and almost all my friends are knitters. That's social. I'm a writer who writes about knitting. That's occupational. And for recreation I, um . . . I knit. I've never quit a job to stay home and knit, although I know someone who called in sick because she was on a hat deadline. Actually, I know lots of knitters who've called in sick to knit, but that's not addiction—that's just the month before Christmas. It's not like they did it so much that they got fired or anything, so that's reasonable. I know regular people who've called in sick and gone to the movies . . . although I also know knitters who have declined to go to the movies with that person because it's too dark to knit there. (Personally, I have mostly solved this by taking plain stockinette socks to the movies. I only have to stay home and knit if I'm at the heel, and that seems normal.) As for declining social events, I don't think the lot of us should be condemned because we'd rather stay home and knit than go to some party, and really, it's not our fault that society is so backward that you feel you shouldn't knit at parties. I understand that staying home to knit is perceived as anti-social, but it's not, really. A lot more of us would take part in social activities if we could use our substance while we were there . . . and with that rationalization, I tick the mental box for that one.

I stop and review for a second, sitting there with the book open on my lap. I run my finger down its pages, counting the criteria that I've said yes to. Five. I've ticked off five, although I really resent number six (it's a coincidence that my whole life is knitting), so let's say it's four. Four is not good, since I only needed three in a year to qualify as substance dependent, which

I had suspected but don't really want to hear. I admit that I'm sort of dependent on knitting, but I do like to think that it's the way that some people are dependent on reading, walking, taking long baths, playing hockey, or breeding small dogs. Everybody has a thing, and just because you would never want to stop doing that thing doesn't mean that you couldn't do without that thing. I can't imagine a life without being a knitter, but if something happened and I wasn't anymore, I'm sure I'd live. (I'm not sure what that existence would look like, but I guess I could try getting a small dog.) There's a missing connection here. How is it that I can tick off all these boxes but remain completely unconvinced that it applies to me? Is it just denial? I know that a lot of my behavior spells addiction or dependence and that if these criteria are all there are to it, knitters, rather collectively, are sunk. Rather dejectedly, I scan the last item on the list.

(7) **The substance use is continued despite knowledge of having a persistent or recurrent physical or psychological problem that is likely to have been caused or exacerbated by the substance (e.g. current cocaine use despite recognition of cocaine-induced depression or continued drinking despite recognition that an ulcer was made worse by alcohol consumption).**

I stare. I reread that one. I stare again, and realize that this is the one. This is the missing piece of the puzzle—how it is that I and every other knitter I know can meet most of these criteria and still insist that it's not a problem in the slightest. I admit that the human ability for denial is pretty remarkable, and that we're all loathe to admit we have a problem, but most of us are pretty quick to identify problems in others, and I can honestly say that I don't feel like my friends and co-knitters (all of whom would have to tick off as many boxes, if not more) have any sort of a problem at all, despite being the poster kids for addictive behavior as it's defined by this collection of doctors and smart people. The whole way down this list of criteria I've been trying to make it fit, trying to accept that you can be addicted to almost anything, and that maybe this really is the same as being addicted to gambling, heroin, liquor, or sex. Maybe (like all addicts) we just don't want to hear about our problems. Now, though, this last item explains everything and takes the heat off entirely.

For something to be a true addiction, for it to be a problem in your life—it has to actually be harming you in some way. It's okay for you (and me) to be filled with glee at the thought of a yarn sale. It's awesome, actually, provided that you aren't knocking over a convenience store for the cash on your way there. A big stash can really just be a supremely good collection of something you're interested in, provided you haven't told the children they have to sleep in a tent in the backyard so Mama has more yarn room. You can be as interested in this as you want, and it's not an addiction until you're trying to score clean needles and some acrylic in an alley, just so you can do a few lines, or are shakily crawling through the broken window at your local yarn shop, because you really, really can't wait until morning. Unless that's you, we're fine.

THINGS TO LEARN

1. Buying yarn to lift my mood will only make me feel better for a little while. Then I will have less money and less space, which is actually less uplifting. This is actually true about almost all shopping.

2. It saves time to take time to do things right. I resent the hell out of that one, because even after almost forty years of knitting, I still can't believe that there's no way to speed this up. I have to admit, though, that after forty years of trying to figure out where to cut corners, it turns out that knitting just doesn't work that way. Cutting a corner means what you make is less good, things that are less good are either less durable or funny looking, and either way people wear that stuff less (or not at all) and then you've totally wasted your time because you have a sweater with one sleeve that sort of puffs because you didn't rip back and have a do over when you totally knew that the short rows were funny, and

now nobody's ever going to wear it. For example. Not that I learned that the hard way or anything.

3. It takes me about sixteen hours to knit a plain pair of sock-weight socks.

4. I do not knit socks full time.

5. Clearly, understanding items 3 and 4, my expectations concerning how much sock yarn I should be buying are way too high.

6. Related to items 3, 4, and 5 above, I may be dangerously delusional . . . since I understand these things and still don't think this means I have too much sock yarn.

7. There is absolutely nothing that can be said to one's employer to properly explain that you have a knitting deadline for your sister's baby and really can't come in to work. I would have better luck getting a day off if I said that all my clothes burned up in a house fire and that coming to work means coming naked.

8. No matter how interesting it is to me, and no matter how long I think about it, I have to admit that knitting probably

moves too slowly to make a good basis for a reality show like *Dancing with the Stars* or *America's Next Top Model*.

9. It is okay to use stash yarn. The integrity of the stash does not need to be maintained. It is not a mine shaft that will collapse in on itself and destroy everything if I take something out.

10. I should not resent it when socks wear out. The average woman weighs 150 pounds and takes between 5,000 and 8,000 steps a day. I should consider it a miracle and be nothing short of astonished if socks last more than a single wearing.

MOTHER'S DAY

I know that I will be voted down by bleeding hearts and sensitive types (and by offspring everywhere who think it's a grand tradition) but I hate Mother's Day. I really do. I've tried my level best to get behind it, especially when society makes such a big deal out of all the cards, but I hate it. I hate it with a burning passion that rivals my hatred of squirrels. (Long story.) As an experienced mother with more than twenty years on my résumé, I'm going on record to say that I would rather be treated decently throughout the year than have my children try to generate a gift not born of a genuine urge to thank me, but more out of an urge not to look like a complete arse on the day designated for mothers. I'm aware that their motives aren't authentic, and it rankles.

When the kids were little, my rage centered around two things. First, it is a grave injustice to set a woman up to have her worth as a mother demonstrated in one heavily loaded day, as in, if you love me you'll do a good job and this day will be smashing, but if you don't love me then I will be able to tell, because this Sunday will be the same as last Sunday when you spilled an entire bottle of syrup on the kitchen floor and did nothing but smear it around with a damp cloth, so we had to worry about the cat getting stuck again. Second, I've always thought it was brutally unfair that Father's Day goes down so much better, mostly because the backbone of Father's Day are the mothers who keep it running right, and that Mother's Day is, much to its detriment, run by fathers and children who don't know that what most mothers want on this day isn't a breakfast in bed that they'll have to pretend to like and clean up afterward, but to stay in bed and read a book, or have a bath without anyone talking to them through the door.

When the girls were really tiny, Mother's Day didn't go well because they were babies, and babies don't care about Mother's Day (or any other day, for the record). They still puke on that day, and they still want only you on that day and you still can't stop them from peeing down your skirt in a restaurant on that day, even though it's been clearly marked to be your day. The most loving spouse can't make a baby not wake you up seventeen times to be nursed on Mother's Day. Intelligent women, myself included, should give up entirely on any Mother's Day involving a human young enough to have no control over their bodily fluids, and lower their standards accordingly.

When the girls were a little bigger, they couldn't focus on it, and if you can't spell "Mother's Day" you probably won't be able to pull if off. Mother's Day is about putting someone else ahead of yourself, and little ones can't do that—and even if they do try, just understanding that it's Mother's Day really isn't enough to stave off the temper tantrum that's inevitable if you are six years old and the card you tried to make is stuck to the table with glue. I let go of those days too, even as I soaked the glue and sparkles off of the table and soothed my child's disappointment by assuring them that I'd never wanted anything more for Mother's Day than sparkles embedded in the carpet and a three-hour cleaning job, and that it was better that the card was stuck on the table. Now I could see it all day long.

When they were teenagers, I'm pretty sure that what went wrong was that simply by their nature, being people who are busy becoming people and therefore not able to pull their heads out of their arses for fifteen seconds, they had some selfish behavior. On one classic Mother's Day, I remember letting go entirely when I told a teenager I'd rather they stayed home and spent time with me that evening, and they turned to me point blank and said that since I was always in charge "every day was Mother's Day" and that they didn't see why they shouldn't even up the injustice by going to the movies with their friends.

It was always a disaster—a terrible disaster—and it took me years to work out that it was a disaster not because they didn't love me, but because I was actually buying into the idea that this was some sort of report card. That if they really cared, this was my children's chance to show me, and that if they really loved me they would do well, or at least be nice to me, or at least not choose today to flush something of mine down the toilet or try to hustle me for twenty bucks so they could go out with their real friends who really cared about them and have some real fun.

I would stand there and think, "How can you treat me this way? It's Mother's Day. It's supposed to be the day that you show me how much you love me, and this is it? This is the best you can do? This is all that you can find in your heart for me? The stupid fight about belly-button piercing? This is what you're giving me?" Then I would dissolve into tears, not understanding the irony in the fact that if there weren't children, and they didn't act like children, I wouldn't need to be a mother, and, then, feelings injured to the point of breaking . . . I'd haul off and cancel the whole thing. (That's right. I'm that woman. The woman who cancels Mother's Day. It's supposed to be about me. I can do that if I want to.) Some years I even preemptively cancelled it, taking my stand in late April.

It wasn't until lately, when my children are big enough to play the game, that it finally occurred to me that the reason Mother's Day didn't sit right with me was because it wasn't about me. It was about the myth of happy mothers, and selling lots of cards and flowers, and it turns out that pinning all your hopes on one day like it was an award with a title called "How Much My Family Loves Me" is pretty stupid. I mean, the children charmed me and were little turds every day. Why attach more significance to what they dish up on one Sunday in May?

Now my children are big, and instead of the ritual gifts I used to get (raise your hand if you have more than one macaroni encrusted juice can pen holder), I'm going to dinner with my three daughters, and they'll likely pay, and one of them will bring flowers, and they'll all toe the societal line, doing everything they're supposed to, and I'll do what I'm supposed to by being flattered and happy, and grateful, and I really, really will be grateful. Not necessarily grateful for the dinner or the flowers, but grateful for children who care enough to get them for me, care enough to arrive, are employed and sensible enough to afford to treat me, and who are sober enough to know it's Mother's Day at all. I will be grateful, and I will be happy, and I will look back and be glad that all of those difficult Mother's Days are behind me. I'll be grateful that nobody's going to puke this Mother's Day, that nobody is going to yell this Mother's Day, that nobody is going to be a sixteen-year-old who screams, "Why do you think it should be about you all the time?" on Mother's Day. Nope. I'll be another of the happy smiling mothers, sitting in a local restaurant with her happy smiling children, her bunch of flowers, being outwardly grateful for the gifts, and inwardly grateful that I don't put much stock in this day, and that none of my kids are in prison.

These are the easy Mother's Days, the ones where the expectations and I have come to a fragile peace. The Mother's

Days that don't end in rage or tears, and the ones where I know that all the other days of being a mother mean more than one Sunday in May, and as far as I'm concerned, the cultural expectations that have a woman who hates breakfast in bed eating one anyway (and then cleaning up the mess afterward) while pretending that she likes it can shove off. The only thing that I miss about those Mother's Days is that the bouquet was a grubby bunch of dandelions and it came with a hand-drawn card that told me that I was loved . . . and then asked for a loan of five bucks to buy me a present.

TEMPORARY TREASURE

I was with Angela when she lost her mitten. It sounds like it shouldn't be a big deal, but it really was, and I know that, now that it's over, Angela thinks of it more as a regrettable incident than an "episode" but I have to tell you, when that woman first realized her mitten had gone walkabout, she came off the rails. Her mittens were, to be fair, really, really beautiful mittens. They were dress mittens, knit to go with her good coat, knit at a fine gauge, on tiny little needles. They had braids on the cuff, that elegant Latvian knitting trick that takes three rows of clever knitting and turns it into the most unlikely of events, and I knew that Angela had made herself crazy working those braids. There were two on each mitten, enclosing a very pretty band of colorwork in delft blue and white. Above the braids they were intricately patterned, with stylized flowers embraced by twining vines. The palms were a pretty geometric pattern that I knew she had divined herself, and the thumbs, the thumbs lay imperceptibly against the palms when you weren't wearing them. They were a work of fine art, no less beautiful than the Mona Lisa, and Angela had worked them carefully and thoughtfully. The colorwork lay perfectly flat without a hint of a pucker, and the tops tapered to a perfectly elegant point. They were the perfect blue to complement her dress coat, and she was as proud of them as she should have been. They were her dress mittens, and they were hard won.

When it looked like maybe one of the pair were misplaced I thought she might be okay, but as we searched and rooted through her belongings it became more and more obvious that if we couldn't find it, she was going to be unreasonable. When all was said and done, and the mitten was deemed gone for good, things got ugly. She cried, she slammed things around, and then we went and got a stiff drink, consorting with other knitters as we told knitting stories like we were veterans back from the war. We spoke of intricate or huge socks worn through, shawls that went through the wash and got felted, mittens that should have been on strings. We all sympathized, but in the back of my mind was one thing I didn't say: I maybe don't mind so much.

Imagine for a moment, an alternate universe where, through a bizarre series of coincidences and inventions, all the knitting you make is permanent. The nefarious clothes moth is extinct— killed in a horrible lavender plague—and the only moths that remain are simply drawn to flames, not knitting. Somewhere along the line someone invented a washing machine so gentle that it can launder the most gossamer shawl without shrinking or mangling, and nobody has ever heard of a sweater sleeve getting caught under the agitator and summarily munched. There is now a fantastic spray that can remove any stain without ever harming any fiber, and someone has been round the whole world with a hammer so there isn't a single exposed nail head waiting to snag your scarf and rip a hole in it. A very clever sort of ribbing is done now, and nobody ever has the trouble of hats getting so loose they fall over their eyes, and that has similarly solved the problem of the bottoms of sweaters eventually giving way and all becoming A-line maternity wear. Yarn doesn't pill, car doors have sensors so that nothing, not even a scarf, can be caught in one, and, due to a terrible frostbite plague in the seventeenth century, mittens are all sacred items that are bonded to their owners. You are given one pair by a high priestess on your sixteenth birthday, and not only has nobody ever lost one, they can't even imagine a scenario where one falls out of your pocket. Were you to suggest it, they would look at you like you just said you're worried about an attack of flying camels. Mitten loss just isn't possible. Just to cover all the bases, let us also say that stealing clothing (even accessories) is now a crime punishable by death, and that a blue laser comes out of the sky and immolates you if you so much as touch someone else's sweater. The blue beam makes no exceptions for sisters, even if they did use your lip gloss and really, really need your green scarf because it is the only thing that goes with their coat.

Nobody has committed a garment-related crime in seventy-four years out of sheer fear.

In this world, think of who knitters are, what their position in society would be. If nothing ever wore out, got a hole, or became ratty looking with time, don't you think that your urge to knit would rapidly make you unnecessary? Inside of a year or two you would pound out everything that a family needed, and then that would be it. In very short order, you'd be some crazed sort of pest that people worked at avoiding. Your proclivity for churning out mittens would be, in a world where they never went away, a nightmare. The people who love you would see you coming with their twenty-third hat, and since they would still have the first twenty-two, still in perfect condition, still taking up closet space, they'd just look at you bearing down on them with another piece of headgear and think, "Holy hell, are you serious? Is there no end in sight, you raving lunatic?" It would be a mere matter of months before you were avoided like the crazy person you would be. You'd eat alone. People would flinch when they saw you coming. Knitters would be feared. Nobody would even consider learning to knit, because knitters would be thought of as no more than magpies, hoarding up pretty things that nobody needs, while those who love them would be forced to smile and nod at the unending onslaught of scarves, sweaters, socks, and mitts. We'd die out, become extinct.

Knitters already have an image problem. People already have a hard time thinking of us as important contributors to the clothing economy, but the truth is that they do need hats, sweaters, mitts, and scarves, and if we give them one before they go to the store (or after they lose or use up the one from the store) then at least we have need on our side. Angela's lost mitten might be a sad, sad thing, with all that work gone forever, but at least now she needs another pair. Truth be told, if she hadn't lost her mitten, if nobody did, then she'd be reduced to a non-essential worker in no time, not to mention what people would think of her exuberantly large stash. Think of how we all love shopping for yarn, making the decisions, picking the colors and patterns. I'm occasionally overwhelmed by all that there is out there, but at least it's not a one-shot deal. I don't have to pick yarn for the one hat my husband will always wear, every day, for the rest of his life. He needs one a year, and that means that buying and making him a hat isn't an intensely loaded thing. Wouldn't you be paralyzed by the pressure if you were only ever making your mum one scarf? Your son one sweater? In a world where Angela doesn't lose a mitten, she doesn't get the pleasure of deciding what the next pair will be and knowing that those will be loved and needed.

I love the temporary nature of knitted things. I know who I am, and I know that if the world's need for my knitting went, my need to knit would not. I know what I would do, too. About the time that people asked me to stop with the regular stuff, I'd get creative. Car warmers. Chair cozies. Panel curtains for large living rooms with high ceilings, carpets, pillows. I know I'm helpless to stop swathing the world in what I love, and so I love that mittens get lost, that socks wear out, that hats get grungy looking, shawls get lost, and that with time, love, care, and wear, most sweaters will eventually look like complete crap. I know that these are mostly things that knitters resent, but, if we look deeply, isn't it a blessing of sorts? How else are we to find a lifetime of work and need—not to mention complete justification for what we've all got going on in the stash.

THAT SORT OF MOTHER

Once, in my career as a mother, I did something so shocking to the other parents and children of my neighborhood that it is still talked about. Even though my daughters are teenagers and a great deal of time has passed since that day, from time to time in the grocery store or when I am in the park, children will point and whisper, and every once in a long while, another mother will gingerly approach me and say, "Excuse me? Was it you? Did you really do that?" When this happens, all I can do is tell the truth. I put my shoulders back, touch her hand, and say, "Yes. It was me. I am that mother."

They are speaking of one afternoon late in August. It was a ripe August day, truly hot and steamy, when camp is over but school hasn't started and everything is in limbo and nobody has anything to do. Actually, nix that. Mothers have plenty to do, and I did. It was my three daughters, Amanda, Megan, and Samantha—then about nine, seven, and four years old—who had nothing to do, or as they put it, "Nothing Good." Every mum's heard that. First they say they have Nothing to Do; then, as a mum, you serve up about forty-nine perfectly good things to do, all of which are rejected on unreasonable grounds. The sun is shining too hard to do chalk drawings outside. Their arms hurt too much to read books, Legos are too slow to build, their sister always messes up their paintings, it makes their eyes hurt to do beads, it's too hot to knit because it makes the yarn sticky (that's an excellent point, actually, but it was lost on me that afternoon). I served up idea after idea. They could get the play-clay and make pretend cupcakes, they could blow bubbles in the backyard in the shade, they could listen to music and color what it looked like. They could do any one of a thousand things I thought up, all of which were miraculous answers to the complaint "There's nothing to do," and the little darlings were against all of them. There were lots of things to do, but none of them were Good.

Now, I am a mother of some experience. I know that if three children under ten have decided that there's Nothing Good to do, I am both doomed and outnumbered, and the best thing to do is make a hasty retreat and hope for the best. Usually really having nothing to do puts Nothing Good to do into perspective, and I find the parties more likely to negotiate after a small period of intense boredom. I told them to think about it, and I went upstairs to sort laundry, put away laundry, or bring a load of laundry down to the washer. (Those of you with wee ones will remember these days, in which everything is defined by the state or amount of the laundry. It's a difficult phase. I once threatened to leave the lot of them for good because they changed outfits seven times a day and landed all wardrobe discards in the hamper. Nobody can be expected to withstand that sort of thing. It's inhumane.) The point is that I went off to wage hopeless battle against something and to let them consider their position.

Very little time had passed, maybe ten minutes, when I heard the giggling start. All three of them, chatting and giggling downstairs. If there had been an incident report filed for how that day went, that moment, the moment when I decided that the giggling meant that things were looking up instead of deciding that things were starting to get weird, that moment would be referred to as "mistake number one." Worse than that, I'm certain that the incident report would also read (in the section under "mitigating factors") that it was rather odd and inexplicable that a mother of my experience did not instantly acknowledge that if three related children of different ages were all giggling and entertained by the same thing, then it was only possible that the thing was a sign of the apocalypse, or at the very least threatened my health, happiness, or property. For whatever reason, I did not realize the danger we were all in at that moment. I did not throw down the stack of pink underpants I was filing in drawers, and I did not run downstairs at a dead tilt to find out what was making them giggle, and so what happened next was a surprise. I blame the heat.

After a very short while (I know it was not very long because I had been working a dried apricot out of the carpet upstairs and by this phase in my mothering I was getting pretty good at that) the giggling erupted into laughter. This caught my attention. Like a mighty cat in the forest, I glanced up from the mashed fruit and cast my gaze toward the stairs, as though I might be able to hear better with my attention focused on the woodwork. My muscles tensed. Happy children, children that happy . . . they are up to no good. I poised for action. The laughter came again and I stood up. I started to move toward the door, just as the laughter erupted into hysterical screams of joy. The girls were suddenly whooping and squealing, laughing breathlessly—laughing in the way that every parent with their wits about them knows can only end in tears. Theirs, yours, the neighbors'—someone is going to be crying when children laugh like that.

I practically vaulted the railing, propelling myself with the urgency that comes of knowing you have missed all the warning signs and have little time to avert total disaster. I was halfway down the stairs when I saw the first thing. The wall at the landing was wet. Water dripped down it, puddling on the floor and running along the baseboards, but I didn't stop long enough to try and figure out how it happened. The water in the hall felt to me like it was going to be more of a tip of the iceberg thing, like the time I couldn't find the goldfish and so I careened into the living room. I stopped. I stopped because what I saw when I entered that room was so unbelievable that I had absolutely no reaction prepared. Now, this is saying something. I am the mother of three very bright, active, and creative children. I am the mother of people who once tried to rappel over the upstairs railing using yarn. I am the mother of children who have tried to use the dryer as a hiding place, children who broke our VCR (actually, it wasn't so much broken as "full"). I am the mother of children who have painted their sheets, cut each other's hair, and longed for adventure. I am the mother of children who have tested me, the mother who owns at least fifty books on discipline (which I have read) and not once, not ever, no matter how much I was surprised, have I failed to come up almost instantly with consequences that were firm, made sense, preserved their self-esteem, and were intended to teach outrageously vivacious beings some damned sense.

This was not the case as I stood in my living room that hot, steamy August afternoon. Here is what I saw. The walls were wet. The couch was wet. The chair dripped water onto the carpet, which (I realized as I stood there) was so sodden that it squished liquidly between my toes. One of the curtain panels had a large circular splash on it, and the window beyond dripped evidence as well. In the middle of this, incredibly saturated themselves, their hair hanging in dripping strings around their little faces (still glowing with the thrill of what they had done) stood my wee girls, each of them poised and clutching—and I can't even hardly tell you how unbelievable I still find this—a fully loaded water balloon.

That alone would be enough to put most mothers over the edge. Three children had a water balloon fight in my house. Worse than that, it wasn't like three children broke into my house and had a water balloon fight; they were my own children. I froze. They froze. What happened next is a testament to my parenting self-control. As images of selling the lot of them into a child labor camp sprang to mind, as I felt my throat fill with anger and screams of unbelievable rage, I counted to twenty-three and took as many deep breaths (I tried counting to ten but a water balloon fight in the house calls for just so much more). When I'd regained something resembling composure, I took a step forward. The carpet sloshed under my feet.

"Unacceptable," I said, as calmly as the white-hot anger would allow me. "You three need towels to clean up this mess. Run. Run quickly." They ran. They fetched every towel in the house and as they mopped it up (and I did the high places—the drips falling onto my back alerted me to the wet ceiling) I didn't say much. Somehow, in my fury, I managed to convince myself that they weren't actually hell-hounds sent to punish me for some of the things I did to my own mother (who was just going to love this) but instead that the girls simply didn't have enough information. Sure, you would think that not whipping water-filled projectiles around the living room was common sense, but these are children. They have no common sense. It's why we don't let them vote, buy firearms, or carry lighters.

When the worst of it was sopped up and the towels were put in the washer (by them, not me) I sat the three of them down on the couch and as water soaked uncomfortably into the bums of their shorts, I explained. I explained that I understood that I had never expressly forbidden water fights in the house, but that I was doing so now. I explained that it was uncool, damaging, and absolutely not anything that civilized people did. Ever. I showed them how wet things still were, and explained that the entire downstairs of the house was going to be wet for several days, as in this sort of humidity, things did not dry well. (I then added that even in lower humidity, I was still entirely opposed to the practice, just in case they thought it was a loophole.) I gave them a list of places that water was allowed to be in our house—the bathtub, the sink, glasses—and, to be clear, I followed it up with a list of places it could not be. Places like the dining room walls, the ceiling, or the brown chair by the window. My tone may not have been entirely calm during this phase, but I did resist the urge to scream "What were you thinking?!" As I mentioned before, I am a mother of some experience. I knew they weren't thinking at all, or that they were thinking something that was so insane that if I had known what it was, it would have put me completely over the edge. All it would have taken was one nine-year-old looking me in the eye and saying something like, "You put water on the table when you wash it, what's the big deal," and I would have taken all of their belongings outside and stood there with the garden hose streaming onto the lot of it while shouting, "How do you like your stuff all wet!" just to show the ingrates what it felt like. (This is not an accepted method for teaching empathy and likely would have been poorly understood by my neighbors.)

I was stern. I was disapproving, and, just like all the parenting books said to, I followed protocol. I told them what they had done was wrong. I told them that it could not happen again, I got them to clean up so that they had reasonable and related consequences for what they had done, and then I told them that they had made me very upset. That it would be some time before I felt right about this, and that smart girls would be getting some books to read and having a little quiet time while mummy went and had a bit of a lie down. (Points to me for not saying "a lie down and six gin and tonics," though that was my impulse.) The ladies got books and sat down angelically to read. I staggered off, head pounding, wondering if this sort of thing ever happened to other mothers. (I bet it does. I think they just keep it a secret.) I lay down on my bed with my eyes closed, keeping an ear out for further mischief from the damp axis of evil allegedly reading Beatrix Potter stories to each other in the kitchen.

If there had been an incident report filed for that day, and frankly I'm still shocked that there wasn't, going to lie down and leaving convicted (if shamed) felons in the kitchen alone would be referred to as "a strategic error of epic proportions." Myself, I've moved through the pain and forgiven myself, and now think of it as a rookie mistake, made because of the burden of parenthood and the fact that I hadn't properly slept through the night in a decade. As I lay there, eyes closed, plotting some sort of teachable moment to install compassion and law-abiding behavior in my daughters, I did not hear them. I did not hear anything at all, and instead of letting that register as a warning, I simply thanked my lucky stars that I'd gotten another thing right. Yes, that's what I did. I lay there, congratulating myself on silence and absolute peace gained through superior and thoughtful parenting. I lay there, in fact, while my daughters realized several things—or so they told me during the debriefing much later, when I could stand to look at them again.

Here is what they realized.

1. There were balloons left over, still in the kitchen drawer.

2. They were in the kitchen with the balloons.

3. There was a tap in the kitchen.

4. Despite everything that I had told them, if I really, really didn't want them to throw water balloons in the house, I would have taken away the balloons. (Point to the nine-year-old on that one. The force is strong within her.)

I will spare you the details of the inevitable scene that followed, and only tell you this. When I started to run after the first splash, I was without thought. I was so angry that I could no longer think. I entered the kitchen at a dead run, confirming with shuddering disbelief that my little daughters, apparently no longer human but transformed to vile demon-spawn, were indeed in a second water-balloon fight happening within the walls of my home. I opened my mouth to say any number of things—none of them kind, civil, or responsible—and as I took a deep breath to unleash the fury I could no longer contain, I really had no idea what sort of things I might do to my children in that moment. Right then, a sky-blue balloon sailed through the air . . . and hit me square in the chest. It exploded on impact with my body, drenched me head to toe, and covered me not just with freezing tap water but also with an almost preternatural sense of calm.

I suddenly knew what I had to do. I did not ask them to clean up and take responsibility. I did not explain what they had done wrong, or attempt to salvage their precious developing senses of self. As I stood there, with a shred of blue latex shrapnel clinging to the edge of my nose, I could feel that I was way past being concerned with imparting life lessons. I realized that I had to do the right thing. I had to save their lives. I picked the evidence off my face. I wiped my dripping forehead, and I said one word.

Bed.

They stared at me for an instant, and then I saw it come over them. They realized that what they did next was going to determine their survival, and their instincts kicked in, and without a single word of complaint or explanation, all three of them filed upstairs smartly at two o'clock in the afternoon, changed into pajamas, and lay motionless in their beds. Not a single child moved, and they remained soundlessly there until an unbelievable seven o'clock the next morning.

If you ask my children now about that day, they all remember it clearly. They remember thinking that at some point I would cool off and come up and get them, talk it through, and forgive them. They remember listening to me come up the stairs at five-thirty, thinking that this was the moment of exoneration, and then being astonished when I wordlessly set plates of supper by their bedsides. Megan remembers the sun shining in her face while she lay there. Amanda remembers feeling guilty. Sam only remembers that the whole water balloon fight thing wasn't her idea, and maintains that she was a baby, drawn into evil by her older, wretched sisters. Not one of them can tell me why they didn't get up. Why not a single one of them challenged the ban, made a break for it, tried to negotiate, or even called out to me to apologize in the seventeen hours that they lay in their beds. I don't know why they didn't either. Think about that. They were nine, seven, and four, and they lay there soundlessly without a single word. I remember that whole afternoon thinking that I should go and make peace with them, and wondering why they didn't call out to me. (Admittedly, every time I thought about going, I was dripped on by more evidence, and that helped me maintain a clarity of vision and resolve.) Mostly what I remember is that the next day on the playground, when all was forgiven and my incredibly well rested children were playing and explaining to the other families why they had missed an evening at the park, that face after face, parents and children alike would turn toward me and stare. I think it was respect, I know it was likely also fear, but I tell you this: They never heard of anything like it again, and I am legend.

AN IRRESPONSIBLE MULTIPLIER

When I was in the seventh grade, I had a real barker of a math teacher. My mother maintains that he wasn't as bad as I recall him, but she wasn't there, day in, day out, and I still remember that sort of madness where a whole class of seventh graders knew without a shadow of a doubt that the man was both sadistic and out of his mind, and there was somehow not a single adult who could see it. (I admit, now that I'm a mother I wonder how often my kids and their friends sit around boggling at my brand of madness, but I try not to think about it.) The point is, this guy was not cut out to be a teacher. He was just too loud, too jumpy, and too high strung. His name was not Mr. Franco, though that's what I'll call him here, to protect his privacy on the off chance that there has been an injustice and he has not yet been struck by lightning. Mr. Franco was a crappy teacher, and I was a crappy math student. I struggled with the concepts at the best of times, but he got frustrated when I couldn't learn, and once he got upset and started yelling, then I got upset and once I was upset I got stupider by the minute. Realizing I was upset further discombobulated me to the point of idiocy and then I couldn't even add, and then Mr. Franco would become crazed and start doing things like slamming rulers against tables, and then one girl always cried. It didn't matter who Mr. Franco was yelling at, or what he was yelling about, this tall girl with the desk behind mine would just suddenly take to a sort of desperate weeping. It was horrible. My mother believes that my difficulty and general lack of good feeling about mathematics began that year, but I know that it's just her maternal love for me that won't let her believe that I've always been terrible at it, even before Mr. Franco gave me the pseudo–post-traumatic stress disorder that crops up and makes the little muscle over my right eye twitch every time I hear the word "multiply" even in a biblical context.

Mr. Franco, in addition to being mean and smelling funny, was also the first teacher to tell me a lie. I was old enough that by then I'd been told lots of lies by other people, and I knew it. That the tooth fairy gave the kid down the street more money than she gave me because Bobby had bigger teeth, that other children loved doing chores and never tried to dodge them, or that it was absolutely normal to have a great aunt who drank milk with rye (equal parts) for breakfast. This, though, this was the first bald-faced lie told to me in a school by someone who was supposed to be in the business of revealing the truth about how things worked. The lie was this: Mr. Franco told me that there was only one right answer to a question. 7 × 7 was always going to be 49 (I think that was the number he said) and he maintained that if you got any other answer, then you were wrong. Absolutely wrong, and he then said (here comes the lie) that mathematics was beautiful because that was always true. One right answer, no exceptions.

Now, I'm not really a "no exceptions" sort of person, which is probably why I was suspicious from the minute he said it (mostly because I was working hard at multiplication and got bizarre answers all the time) but the older I get, the more I come to completely understand that he was wrong. The world is simply not that black and white, even when it comes to math.

Knitters engage in math all the time. If you're going to start designing stuff or altering patterns or thrusting your own ideas from yarn to reality, then you're likely going to get in pretty thick with it, but even habitual number avoiders like me will find that even with diligent effort, it's just about impossible to knit and not do any math at all. When a pattern tells you to increase fourteen times evenly across seventy stitches, there's almost no way out of it without doing simple division ($70 \div 14$ = one increase every five stitches). Similarly, if you want to make a scarf and use a particular stitch pattern, one with a repeat of fifteen stitches, you're going to have to be able to add fifteen together enough times to get the width you'd like to have. (Don't forget the addition you'll need to do to add stitches for the edges, and then the subtraction when the thing is inevitably wider than your neck.) Even if you're not doing math computations, mathematic concepts start cropping up where you least expect them, and I'm not even talking about simple math. Knitting math is higher math. Math of a philosophical nature. Math they talk about in lecture halls in universities with ivy on them. Math I will try to explain now, although remember, Mr. Franco's seventh grade class took a terrible and permanent toll on me. If you're a math teacher reading this, cut me some slack.

Let's start with gauge. Gauge is the problem child of knitting mathematics. In its simplest form gauge should work, which is to say that if a knitter reads that she needs six stitches to the inch, knits swatches with assorted needle sizes until she bloody well gets six stitches to the inch, and then uses that needle size and that yarn to make a sweater, then that sweater should (possessing the required gauge) be exactly, precisely the size that the pattern predicts. This is, in mathematics, called a deterministic system. That's a system where if you do the same thing with the same stuff under the same circumstances, you always get the same result, because there's no randomness in it. Multiplication works that way. If you take seven groups of seven and put them together, then you are always, always, cross my heart and hope to die, sell my best merino, going to get the same answer. (That dare on the stash might be going too far. I've already said my math isn't good enough to risk it on my skills.

There will be some knitter with a PhD in multiplication who takes it from me on some technicality.) Gauge should, since it's only a version of multiplication, work exactly the same way, but here's where it falls apart.

Any knitter, even without the help of a single day in a mathematics classroom, can tell you that gauge lies. Lies like a rug. Lies like a four-year-old just caught alone in the bathroom with the family cat. (Hint: Look for the scissors.) We have all had the experience of carefully and precisely getting six stitches to the inch, just like the pattern said, then casting on exactly as many stitches as the pattern said to and then promptly getting a sweater that is either so surprisingly small that you wouldn't put it on a streetwalker and think her appropriately covered, or so large that right after you put it out on the line to dry a family pulled up in a minivan, stuck a tent pole under the right shoulder, tossed four sleeping bags under the belly of it, and started a campfire. What happened? You added six to six as many times as you were told, and the answer should always be the same, right?

I should be very fond of math. I like control, I like predictability, I like knowing what is going to happen and when, and most math is like that. In mathematics, 2 + 2 is always going to be 4. The Pythagorean theorem never changes; it is always $a^2 + b^2 = c^2$, no matter how many times you do it. It doesn't even matter if you don't know what it means; it's still the same.

Most math rules are so hard and fast that if you get another answer, then you know that you've made a mistake. It took me four years of grade ten math (I had some trouble with success on that one) to learn that math at all levels is about trying to figure out what the general rules are. I find this idea really comforting. As difficult as I find computational math to be, at least there aren't an infinite number of answers. If you are a mathematician, there are some things in the world that you just know are true. They are unchangeable, unshakable truths—unlike a philosopher's theories, or an artist's imagination, or a minister's faith, mathematicians get to deal in what they can prove.

Despite being sold to us as a purely deterministic system, gauge, it turns out, isn't. If a philosopher finds something that doesn't work the way it should, they wonder if it is another idea, a theory. They acknowledge that there is much in this world that they do not know yet, and they begin the process of examining the mystery to unravel what might lie behind it. They can resign their misunderstanding and trust in their faith that it makes sense somewhere else. If an artist sees something that doesn't work the way they expect it to, it opens up a world of possibility, where any answer can work if you can draw, sculpt, or paint it. If a minister encounters something that they aren't expecting, like a busload of nuns going over a cliff, they can say it is an act of God, something that has a purpose that is only understood by a higher, more complex power. In math, it turns out that if a mathematician encounters a deterministic system that isn't being deterministic they know that they are now dealing in chaos math.

Chaos math, my friends, is when a system is extremely sensitive to the conditions around it, and that sensitivity has an influence that is so profound that it becomes pretty much impossible to predict what might happen anymore. The Butterfly Effect is like this. Ray Bradbury wrote a short story ("A Sound of Thunder") in 1952 in which a group of time travelers accidentally killed a prehistoric butterfly, and that one tiny change was enough to ripple through time and mean that they returned to a very, very different place from the one they left. One little change in the initial conditions, one tiny thing that you can't see, hear, or imagine influencing the rest of the system, and even though technically that system is deterministic, now there's no way to know how it will all end. It's no longer predictable. It has become chaos. (For the record, to my way of thinking, it seems that once a system is chaotic, it can't be deterministic anymore, but mathematicians now call this deterministic chaos, which only goes to show you how much I have yet to learn, and how likely I am to get a lot of letters from mathematicians about this essay.)

Knowing what we know now, gauge starts to make sense, doesn't it? In a deterministic system, the answer is only predictable if you can repeat the identical system. A billiard ball will only land in the same pocket of the table if it is hit in the same way, precisely, every time. If there's a wind, if a drunk bumps the table, if the ball has dirt on it . . . voilà! Chaos. The system is still predictable, sort of, but only if you know about the dirt, the wind, or the drunk, and can precisely predict their behavior too. This, my darling and clever knitters, is exactly what's happening with gauge. Sure, ten stitches make an inch. That should mean, if the system was purely deterministic, that thirty stitches would be three inches, and one hundred stitches ten. You and I, though, we know that whether or not that actually happens is a total crap shoot, and now we can be comforted by knowing that gauge is actually deterministic chaos. You are human. You cannot possibly do things precisely the same way every time. Occasionally, some stitches are going to be imperceptibly looser than the others, because you relaxed a little, or had a glass of wine. A few others are going to be tighter, because you were on the bus or your spouse tried to tell you again that they are absolutely cleaning the cat box every day, when you know that absolutely isn't true and are considering getting nanny-cam footage to prove it.

How about the fact that the tens of thousands of stitches in a sweater are heavier than the few in the swatch? What impact does that have on a sweater as a whole? I measure all my swatches on the table, horizontally, but when I wear them I'm almost always vertical. Will there be stretch? How much?

Are there seams? The swatch didn't have seams, and that could change everything. Did you wash the swatch? You're going to wash the sweater, and the yarn might relax, tighten up, bloom, explode—anything could happen.

All of this, all of these little, tiny things seem so trivial when you're holding a swatch. They seem like they won't matter at all, but something like mis-measuring your gauge by one eighth of a stitch, for knitters . . . That right there is the flap of the butterfly's wings. That tiny moment, where you missed a fraction of a stitch, that inconsequential thing that, really, you couldn't even have known you were doing, that right there is magnified, rippling ever outward until all you're left with is a broken shadow of a knitter weeping softly in a corner holding a couple hundred dollars' worth of cashmere that's supposed to be a snappy little twin set, yet is something closer to elephant lingerie.

You know what this means to knitting? To have insidious influences creeping into your deterministic system? It means you don't have a deterministic system anymore. You have deterministic chaos, and the important word there is chaos. The only reasonable thing to do with a chaotic system is to realize that it's no longer predictive. You can't know the outcome. Not completely. Doing a gauge swatch will give you valuable information (probably), but it also might lie like a rug, and now you can stop feeling angry or incompetent when that happens. This math thing takes you entirely off the hook. You can't predict all of the factors that will come into play—it's just not possible. It's like expecting to know what a two-year-old might put up her nose or what a teenager sees in that pierced guy. You'll never know, and trying to know will just make you insane. It is better, much better, to acknowledge that now you understand what's going on with gauge. It isn't a purely deterministic system, and any knitting teacher who tells you otherwise is just shining you on, or she's encountered one of the possibilities in a chaotic system, which for her, just once, when everything was exactly in her favor and she didn't know it, worked, and that one time has convinced her it's possible for it to happen again. What we do know is that there is no chance that people like her haven't been burned by this. They're either in denial because of the pain, or they're keeping it a secret to appear superior. You know the truth. You know in your heart that gauge is simply an irresponsible multiplier. There are forces at work when you knit that are mysterious, deep, and mathematical.

Is 7×7 always 49, as Mr. Franco told me in grade seven? Nope. Not even close, and I have a hat so small it won't cover a baseball to prove it. Seven times seven is usually forty-nine, but, in knitting, it could be forty-eight, fifty-two, or six. Accept it, and know that knitting would have made Mr. Franco crazier than a one-needled knitter at a yarn sale.

THE POINT SYSTEM

$\mathcal{T}$here is an unfinished sweater in my closet. Actually, that statement is sort of untrue. There are several unfinished sweaters in there, but most of them have a fate that's sealed. They will never be finished sweaters. It has been my experience that every once in a while a particular yarn and pattern combination has an effect that culminates in the project equivalent of a terminal illness, and, despite the best of intentions and through no fault of the knitter, it can't work. The sweater has the wrong gauge, it doesn't look right, the yarn obscured the cables, you realized that you must have been drunk when you bought that shade of green because even knitting it makes you look like you've contracted a tropical disease with permanent consequences . . . something happens and it tips the project over into that abyss where you know it won't ever be finished, but it won't be ripped back either. Those projects sit in the closet, marinating with the other yarn and stash, and it doesn't bother me at all. Every now and then I go into the stash for something else and I see those projects, and there is no pang of guilt, no feelings of loss or failure, no negative feelings at all. I mean, I wish they were finished sweaters; It would be great if they were finished sweaters, especially if they could be finished sweaters without the problems that consigned them to the closet in the first place, but it all just sort of feels like having those sweaters is impossible. It's like seeing a woman in her forties who has perky breasts, is a steady size zero, and struggles not to be "too thin." It's just not something that's ever going to be in my life and I don't even expect it. The unfinished sweaters and I are pretty reconciled to each other.

Right now, though, there's one in there that's lurking at me. I don't know any other way to explain it. I know it's there, because it's practically oozing out a frequency of guilt and abandonment that I can feel all the bloody time. I walk by the closet, and I don't even have to see it; I just know that it's in there, and I feel terrible about it. See, the sweater in the closet isn't terminal. It was going pretty well when I put it in there, and it turns out that it is one thing to put a sweater that you know is never going to make it onto a metaphoric ice floe and watch it drift out to sea, but to wander off from a sweater that's got nothing wrong with it . . . it's not a mercy killing. It's just murder, and that makes me feel guilty.

I've been trying to figure out for weeks what happened between me and that sweater. What snapped in me that made me take the thing, bundle it up with its needles, and shove it into the back of the closet. I know I can be a pretty unfaithful knitter, but really, a project has to at least give me a reason before I go. I don't usually dump a good sweater like yesterday's coffee grounds unless there's at least a better sweater on the horizon, but this time it was very cold and calculating. I just put it in a jumbo Ziploc and walked away. Didn't see a better yarn that made this one look ratty, didn't find a new pattern that looked like a thrill a minute, didn't have a buttonhole come out too big and give me an excuse. The yarn didn't bug me, the pattern didn't have an error, it wasn't time to do the buttonbands. (I hate buttonbands. A truly civilized world would have found a way past them. That's all I'm saying.) Nothing happened, I was knitting along, everything was going well, and then I just snapped, stuffed it in a bag, and consigned it to the closet as if it was where the thing was born to be.

In the beginning, the relationship between that sweater and me was so charmed that if there were sweater knitting romance movies, we would have gotten the leads. I got gauge perfectly, bang on, the first time I tried. I took my wee swatch and washed it to see if the gauge stayed the same, and it did. The yarn didn't change at all—didn't bloom and get bigger, didn't have the body wash out of it and suddenly turn up flaccid. There was no change at all, except that the yarn was wet and then it dried. Then I started knitting and the yarn was plain and good, worked perfectly well, was comfortable in my hands and made a nice fabric. It was neither too flimsy nor too bulky. It was exactly as I had hoped it would be. As I continued, the pattern was accurate and clear, and the pattern writer had thoughtfully put any difficult or unexpected directions in the proper order so that there wasn't even a chance I would miss an instruction and screw up. I carried on, and as I did I measured, and I'll be damned if the thing wasn't coming out exactly the right size. I even, and I cannot stress enough how unlikely and unbelievable this is, I even got both row and stitch gauge. That never happens. Until that moment I actually thought that achieving row gauge was an urban legend, like alligators in the sewers, or cats sucking the breath out of babies. I have heard of it, people talk about it, but nobody can ever show me an example, and stories of people getting both kinds of gauge always seem to happen to a friend of a friend. I've simply never seen it, and here it was, effortlessly turning up on this perfect sweater that was going wonderfully well. I can't stress this enough. There were no problems with that sweater, not a one, and unlike its deformed, unlucky, and misadventured brethren already in the closet, I think maybe that's why it got the chop. It was going so well, so wonderfully well, so completely without incident, so painfully undistinguished in its ordinariness, that frankly, the whole thing just about makes me weep casual tears of tepid boredom to think of it.

This realization may mean that I have figured out something important. I've hung in there with sweaters that have pulled all kinds of crap on me. I have had whole sweaters pull terminal stunts on me mere centimeters from finished, and I have still completed the sweater. You wouldn't believe what I'll put up with. I have been the victim of some knitting-related crimes that would have resulted in life sentences for the yarn involved, were it not inanimate. (It is extremely difficult to prove motive and intent for a crime if everyone keeps telling you that the perpetrator isn't alive.) I've re-knit a neckline upwards of seven times, but this sweater is pleasant to me and it gets the chop? The evidence is pointing to a slightly troubling conclusion. It turns out that I might be the sort of person who likes my projects to be trouble, or difficult, or to mess me up for sport, and what, really, does that say about me? This project wasn't hurting me; it was nothing but vague pleasure, and I dumped it. It would seem that I like my knitting to jerk me around more than a little, and I have to stop and wonder if I am the knitting equivalent of a masochist—someone who's enjoying taking a challenge too far and now only likes it if it hurts.

I thought this over and realized that, really, I *don't* like knitting to hurt me. True, I've stuck with yarn that seems bent on deliberately crushing my spirit, but there are lots of projects in the back of the closet that ain't never seeing the light of day again because they obviously had an antagonistic nature and no intention of becoming a sweater. They were projects that crossed an invisible line and took it too far, and they got canned and stuffed in a Ziploc for the offense. Their presence in long-term incarceration has got to mean that I do have some sense of self protection, which is somewhat comforting. If, however, I've been known to can a project for either being too much trouble or too little challenge, I must be operating in a range, a mystical, magical zone of satisfaction where the knitting scores enough points somehow to stay in my zone of acceptability without crossing over into a place where it rises above challenge and into the realm where it's personally stupid to continue.

I've wondered at something like this before. Perhaps what's happening is a highly personal interest and ability threshold. Like how we all choose a plain knit if we're going to be watching a complex movie. This is partly because the movie will have most of our interest, but I suspect that it's as much for the sake of the plain knit. Unless you're a particularly meditative person, most of us think of the idea of a huge, plain, garter stitch blanket with some sense of creeping ennui. Once you're past the beginner phase of knitting, it's just not enough of a challenge for your clever mind. If we were to add up its points toward that interest/ ability threshold, an ocean of garter stitch is going to score a one on the scale of challenge. This doesn't mean that you won't knit it; it's just that now it needs something added to it to bring it up to your minimum level.

After careful reflection, I think my personal minimum score for anything I'm thinking about doing—knitting or not—is about a seven on the interest scale. If something's scoring a five, like a movie, then I need to add at least two points of knitting to it for me to be able to hang in. If it's something gripping, like a conversation with a charming and entertaining friend, I may not need to add much knitting at all. If my friend scores a nine, I might only toss in a plain sock, with no patterning or anything, just round and round on autopilot while we visit. (I can only think of one thing I do with another person that really has no room to add any sort of knitting to, but let's not discuss it here.) A plain sock by itself is terribly boring, but it could score points by having a clever stitch pattern, or maybe by being made out of a very beautiful yarn that's an enchantment to work with. (Sadly, it is still infuriatingly true that being beautiful without being clever is almost always worth more points than being clever without being beautiful, but such are the rules of life and knitting—they are cruel, but there anyway.)

We all stomp around with our knitting, assessing whether or not it's enough to hold our interest and then adding whatever points the thing can't provide. Reading a book while you knit, listening to music, watching a movie, adding a friend. . . . or removing one if we need to. We've all knit something fussy enough, so high on the interest scale, that to get through it, nobody was allowed to speak directly to you. I once worked a start to a shawl that was so high on the interest scale that I silenced the family, locked myself in my room with a calming cup of tea, and still just about blew out the section of my brain I use for counting, screwed up three times, and came down with a shake. Everybody has their own threshold, deeply personal and intimate, and this sweater, the perfect sweater, just didn't come near mine. It wasn't enough of a challenge, and there was nothing I could add to it that would bring it up to the point where it could stay.

This theory means (rather comfortingly) that it isn't at all that I enjoy pain. It's instead a universal part of the way the human brain is wired. Human beings are the only animals that seek challenge. All other mammals respond to a challenge if it's presented to them or because they need to, but we are the only animals to seek danger, adventure, and challenge for fun. We are the only species that is able to put interests that are not genetic out front. I assure you, there's no way that a fellow mammal would understand the urge to run a marathon for no reason other than the feeling of accomplishment it gave you. The local band of mammals would want to sit you down and ask you what the hell was wrong with you. How could you waste all those calories? You don't know when your next meal is walking by or ripening, and here you are, running for no reason so that you're too tired to protect yourself? Aren't you worried a lion will eat you? They'd stare at you with wonder, trying to figure out why on Earth you would be making your life so much harder than it had to be. Imagine the look an antelope would give you if you tried to explain skydiving for a thrill. We're the only species that invents all of this stuff to make our lives easier—like a car so that we don't need to walk—then invents something else to take the place of it, like running on a treadmill. We're challenge junkies. Our bright, vivid minds mean that we want and need things to do, and that they need to be challenging and interesting. If we replace bright, active, challenging activities like hunting and gathering with mundane, unfulfilling activities like going to the grocery store and watching TV, then we've got to find a way to up the ante for ourselves, and we have to add stuff to up the interest level without making ourselves crazy with overwork. We are the only species that aspires. The only species that dreams of making beautiful things. That dares to try to be better than we were before, to aim higher, to cable where once we could only do garter stitch. We're unique among the animals, and it's not that we like things to be miserable. The sweater didn't get the boot for being miserable. It was kicked to the back of the closet for being . . . well, boring, and humans hate boring.

We, as knitters and as people, are all looking for our own deeply personal middle ground. We hate jobs that are boring and are demoralized by things that are genuinely too difficult, but watch us magnetically slink over to something that can hold our interest and challenge us without becoming too punishing. Watch us, if we can't find that thing—watch us create it. Watch us take a boring thing and make it tolerable by adding another layer. We put on a movie while we knit garter stitch. We take a sock for a boring commute. Confronted with something that's not a challenge, something too perfect, we deliberately up the ante right to the spot just before it has to go to the closet for being too hard, and if we can't get it there, then it could get the closet for that too. Personally I think I can prove this with my choice of a husband. Now that I understand why that beautiful sweater hit the showers, I think I know how my Joe is keeping this marriage going. I'm staying with him because he's constantly walking the fine line where he's challenging enough that I'm interested in him, but not so challenging that I end the relationship because he's' driving me beyond wild and into crazy. He and I have a lot of conversations about where that line is, and how he might want to keep his eye on it. I keep him even though he drives me wild, because humans have unique brains. We like a challenge. We have an intrinsic love of hard work (though I find it hard to believe when the work ahead of me is cleaning, but I suppose every theory has its sticking points) and we will add interest to an activity to make it more challenging, right up to our own personal threshold. Therefore, I maintain that I boosted a boring sweater into the back of the closet not because I lack stick-to-itiveness or the ability to follow through, but because my brain is a wonder, I have a need to be challenged, and I was, frankly . . . too much of a human to knit that sweater.

UNTIL WE MEET AGAIN

𝒟ear Second Wrap Cardigan,

I feel terrible writing this to you, but I have to.

I'm leaving you. Right away. I'm going to ravel your knitting, wind you back into balls, and pass you along to another knitter so that there can be some sort of future for you, because I assure you, there isn't one here.

I know that you're going to think this is harsh, and perhaps unfair, and who knows, maybe it is. I just know that I can't work it out with you. I've tried, heaven knows I've tried, but all this time we're spending together is a lie. You're just not ever going to be a sweater that I like, and I can't keep knitting on you like that's not true, because it just gets both of our hopes up that someday there will be a real garment between us, and it's time that we both admit that's never going to happen.

I wish I could define the certain something, the thing or the moment that's coming between us, but the truth is that I just hate your stinking guts. I've tried not to hate you, but despite how millions of couples are staying together for the sake of the children, a relationship filled with hate just isn't something I need to do, because, dude, you're yarn. Just yarn, and I've got lots more where you came from.

If it seems to you like I've led you on, I apologize. I know it's been confusing. I did buy you. I did stand in that yarn shop in New York City on a beautiful spring day, and I did look at you, knit up into that wrap cardigan, and I did say, "Wow, I freakin' love that sweater." I did say it. I even remember saying that I thought you would look great with jeans. I know I said it, I know you have witnesses. The thing is, I think maybe I had wine with lunch that day, or maybe I was coming down with something, because now that I have you here in my hands, I cannot, for the life of me, figure out what I saw in you. You're pretty colors, I give you that, but—and I'm sorry if nobody's mentioned this to you before—you're a novelty yarn. I tried to pretend it's not true, but you are.

You've got a big stinking bobble on your strand every thirty centimeters, and I don't know how to talk about that. I thought when I saw you that the bobbles were interesting. I thought you were funky. I thought you were hip and fun, and I didn't just overlook your bobbles, standing in that yarn shop, I embraced them. Now that we've been together a while, I can't explain what I was thinking. I am not funky, or hip, and I think jeans and a clean T-shirt should be acceptable clothing for every occasion, and what's further, I've never seen a reason to own more than one bra and four pairs of shoes, and that counts skates. What about that vision says "funky" to you? When people talk about accessorizing, I think about carrying a cup of coffee. Is that hip? No. No, my woolly friend, it's not, and why on Earth some other feeling came over me while I was in that shop is beyond me. (I blame New York. There's something about that place that makes you imagine you could dress better, and it's best not to shop while you're conflicted like that. It's just confusing).

I know that after that day, the day that I stood in that shop, admired the sample, and then bought you, the friend I was with was skeptical. She didn't say it, but I know what she was thinking. She was trying to figure out how a woman who wonders whether her outfit is too "flashy" if it has buttons was really going to reconcile herself to a handpainted, multicolored, bouclé yarn with bobbles strung along it. I could tell that my friend saw it then that it wasn't going to work, and some of these evenings that we've been together, you and I, the ones where I look at you and I think, "How did I end up with you and, my God, when will we stop pretending to like each other," I wonder why she didn't say something. Why she didn't steer me straight past you and say, "This is like when you wanted to date Prince. He looks like a lot of fun but we both know it would end up pretty freaky"? That's what friends should do for each other. Long before it all ends with tears, a bottle of Shiraz, and a ball winder ripping back a relationship, your friends should come to you and tell you they think this yarn won't work. They know me well enough to know that any sweater plan that begins with a novelty yarn and ends with the intention of something I would wear is a frank impossibility. Why didn't they say something before you and I got serious? At knit night, at the shop, why not a few words sometime when I came in without you? The whole lot of them could have said, "Hey, Steph, that yarn isn't for you. It's got bobbles, and you know how you feel about that," and then maybe I would have said, "Holy cow, you're right. I remember the last time I had bobbly yarn. I made fun of it for knitting up into a surface that made it look like I had a million nipples on my chest. Right you are. Thank you for saving me all that time and money. You guys are great!"

I know, though, that it wouldn't have worked. If my knit-sisters had taken a moment and said something about how you were as matched to my taste as nude go-go dancing in public is, I would have told them that they were wrong. That you were charming, and fun, and that it was time to embrace something a little different and try new things, and isn't it okay, just once in a while, not to be yourself entirely? That maybe there is something wonderful about stepping outside of what you always like, what you always do, who you always are. I know that I have nineteen plain brown shirts and, I admit it, I do think they look really good with plain brown pants (and for the record I think the way I put that look together has way more flair than a UPS man's uniform), but does that really mean that I wouldn't look fabulous in a multicolored, bouclé, bobble yarn, wrap sweater? Does it really? Just because this is who I am now, does that mean that I can't grow? Can't change? Can't knit and love a yarn that isn't really me?

If they'd have told me that you were wrong for me then, I wouldn't have seen it. Love is blind, my skeined buddy, and just like it is with anything you're dumping, the time for your friends to tell you, "I've always hated him and I knew from the start that it could never work" is after the breakup, when the yarn is gone for good.

In any event, I'm mostly sorry. Not hugely sorry, because, as I believe I mentioned before, you are actually only yarn and you're actually inert. It was just me who got crushed. As much as it feels like you were a part of this process and this relationship, you never made an effort. I got my time wasted and learned that my self-image isn't quite ready to make the leap from beige to bobbles. I got taunted by the promise of a cute new sweater that's not going to happen, and you . . . you're what you started out as. You're a fine-looking yarn with bright promise, who's going to make some other knitter very happy someday, when you're away from me.

That other knitter, she'll knit you up into something, probably a funky wrap cardigan, just like I tried to make, and every time a bobble shows up she'll be thrilled instead of secretly and intensely horrified that a bobble yarn is making bobbles. When it's done she'll be cozy and delighted, and she'll wear you everywhere and the two of you will be totally happy together. Yes, that's how it will be. I'll put you down and pick up with a really traditional tweed in some shade of brown and that yarn and I will make some cables together, and you'll go find a fun-loving knitter who embraces you for what you are. In time, we'll both move on, and this time we've spent, when we both knew the truth and I kept knitting anyway, this horrible few weeks when we were together all the time and couldn't tell each other the truth, will all be a memory. We'll remember that you wanted me to be something I wasn't, and I wanted the same thing from you, and in time, we'll forget about each other.

Years later, one day in spring, I'll be walking down the street, probably while visiting New York, when the cherry blossoms are out in Central Park and it's all so romantic, and I'll pass someone on the sidewalk. It will be a woman who looks fantastic. She'll be tall and gorgeous, probably wearing black skinny jeans and tall black boots, and she'll have on a black scarf that trails gossamer behind her. She'll be walking with authority, probably laughing with her friends on the way to cocktails, and she'll be so sexy, and so chic, and she'll look so incredible that I'll wish I was her, and that's when I'll see it. She's wearing you—a multicolor, bouclé, bobble-knit wrap sweater—and your strand will make her look like she's got a million nipples, only, on her, a million nipples look fantastic.

In that minute, I'll miss you and what we could have been, if only we were ready for each other.

Cheers, and best of luck.

Stephanie

OCTOBER

I have always had a thing for October. It is my favorite month of the year, I think, and I am pretty sure that it is because of the leaves turning color and falling, carpeting almost all of my world with a beautiful rustling blanket. I know it might not be so where you live, but my country is Canada, and while this country does a lot of things very well that I am truly proud of, it would seem that we sort of specialize in forests and autumn splendor. I live in Ontario, a province so big that you can drive for twenty-four whole hours at a good clip, without stopping, and still not be in another province yet. Ontario is more than a million square kilometers (more than 415,000 square miles) of area which is, for reference, about one-sixth the size of the entire lower forty-eight states of America. Despite its size, a remarkable thing about this place is that no matter where you are it won't take you long at all to get to a forest. Even here in the city of Toronto, a city teeming with millions of people, I can be communing among the trees a few minutes' walk from my house, and, in October, that's where you'll find me much of the time.

When I was a little girl I read a story in a book about a Japanese boy who was asked to prepare the path for an important visitor. I wish I still had the book so I could tell you exactly what it was called, but I remember the story so clearly. The path was partially covered with cherry blossoms, and the little lad painstakingly swept it clear, and then called his teacher to come and check his work. His teacher looked at that path and told him it wasn't good enough, and the poor little kid swept it again, this time more carefully, before the teacher told him again that it wasn't up to snuff. In the story, this went on for a while, with the kid cleaning up more and more of the cherry blossoms while his teacher waited for him to figure out that preparing the path meant shaking more of the beautiful blossoms onto the path, since there were only a few days of the year that it was possible to have such a beautiful thing. When I first read that story, I really thought that letting the kid spend a whole day sweeping a path before you told him that all of his efforts were pointless was pretty damn rude of the teacher, but I've sort of gotten over it now that I understand better. Every October as I walk through the leaves on the sidewalks, parks, driveways, and paths, I think about that story, and it makes me reluctant to rake up that wonderful carpet and occasionally inspires me to tell a total stranger to consider leaving their leaves on the ground, just for a few days. (It is well noted that this never occurs to me in spring when there are actually cherry blossoms, but such are the wonders of my mind.)

As I rustle and stomp and swish through the leaves, I realize that I love the way that October sounds. Not the word October, but the sound of the month itself. I guess if I were a thief or a ninja or another sort of person who needed to creep around silently for professional reasons, the fall would really get to me, but since I'm not a ninja, I just love it. The leaves on the ground are inviting. I hear that sound under my feet and it makes me want to put on a sweater and go for a walk, and, oh—the sweaters, they are simply the thin edge of the wedge when one begins to describe October.

October is unequivocally the best month of the year for a knitter in these parts. Sweaters, scarves, shawls, and hats . . . they all come out and make glorious solo flights. In just a few weeks sweaters and scarves alone won't be enough. A coat will cover my glorious sweater, my hood will be pulled up over my hat, and the beautiful scarf I'm showing off will be tucked in tight, caulking against the snow and ice, holding back the fierce winter. In October though, a sweater is just the thing, and I believe that this has a tremendous influence on the non-knitting population and their thoughts about knitters. Walking through the leaves and downtown streets of my city in this month, I always think that people must see my handknit beauties and wish, if only for that glorious moment, that they too were so lucky as to be a knitter. (It has been pointed out to me, as I don a sweater, hat, scarf, and mittens—all my very best—that it's more likely that they're wondering who that lady is wearing all the knitted stuff, but this is my fantasy, and I like it the way it is.)

In October, my lone kitchen houseplant has dropped a few leaves, just trying to join in, and in October, I am always so consumed by knitting and how wonderfully appropriate it is to have wool around that I have always considered knitting my children's Halloween costumes. (Sadly, it is never my good sense, but their lack of desire for a knitted costume, that has stopped me.)

In October, you never say just, "It's a lovely day." That's what you think in September, but in October, it's always followed by the wistful thought, "Too bad there aren't very many left," while sighing exactly as though the world ends when the snow flies. October sunshine is made sweeter by there being a little less of it every day, because every day in October the daylight has a harder time starting in the morning and the night creeps in a little sooner in the evening. In October, it's a little cooler each day, and the retreat of the light and warmth of the sun makes it feel like what October sunshine remains isn't to be missed.

One day, when October is almost run out, almost ready to give way to the far more depressing pallor of gray November, I am out on my fourth walk of the day, just so I can hear and see October, when I notice that the leaves aren't changing anymore—they've changed. I turn and look for a locust tree, always the last guy to drop his leaves, and I see it nearly naked against the bright clear sky, and it hits me. It's almost not fall anymore, it's almost winter, and I stand there in the leaves and realize that soon it will be the long dark time, and I'll have to wait months—six or seven—before the trees are awake, before leaves are part of my world again.

That same day, I saw a little kid running in my park (I think of it that way in October), and he was piling up leaves as high as he could. When the pile was as big as any of imagination, he would back up, trying to run backward, mostly failing, laughing already in anticipation of his launch. Face shining, when he thought he had enough distance, he'd run at the leaves full tilt, giggling madly, and then all in a riot, he'd dive into the mountain of leaves, the rustling deafening, his grin wicked. He was wearing a bright blue handknit sweater, a little bit too big for him, and it was perfect. The whole scene was perfect. That little kid, with his black hair and his blue sweater, running and playing in the orange, yellow, and red of the leaves. It was heartbreakingly beautiful.

How many Octobers does a person get? How many times do you watch your trees put on and shrug off their fiery best? How many chances are there to rake the leaves onto the path, rather than off it, to enjoy all that October offers? Seventy Octobers? Eighty? I stood in the leaves, the orange and red leaves bright against the beautiful sky, and the little boy in the blue sweater ran by me and entirely buried himself in his pile of leaves, laughing so hard that even his breaths were made of giggles. This is maybe . . . his fourth October. I bet it's the first one he'll remember.

Watching him, I could think only one thing: I should totally knit a blue sweater.

FAILURE TO THINK

I make a lot of mistakes, not just in knitting, but all over the place, and mostly I don't mind a lot. I'm pretty sure that I'm making this many mistakes because I'm actually trying new things and learning new stuff all the time, and experience is a great teacher, even if it leaves a little embarrassment and humiliation in its wake. Mostly, except for the humiliation and embarrassment, I've grown accustomed to the sort of mistakes I usually make, the things that happen when you're not sure how something works, and you try, make a mistake, and then after that know what you're doing. Like the time I filled a house full of smoke because I made a mistake with a wood stove. There was nobody there to teach me whether the flue was open or closed, I had a fifty–fifty shot at getting it right, and I was wrong. I lit the fire, the smoke billowed into the room, and I had the information I needed about the flue. It was definitely closed. That was absolutely a valuable mistake—just like the time that I saw the PTA lady headed my way on the playground. I knew that woman was going to try to rope me into volunteering for a school function; I knew I didn't have time to help, but I also knew that I was going to be absolutely helpless in her grasp. I looked into my future and saw that my inability to say no was absolutely going to end with me baking 324 cupcakes at three in the morning and I decided to run. There was an excellent chance it would have worked too. I could have shouted, "Sorry, Marie, no time," and whipped off home, safe and sound, bake sale free—but that's not what happened. What happened is that I made a mistake. I tried to run away too quickly, I didn't look around me well enough, and when I panicked and turned to run it just so happened that I ran into a tree, knocked myself down, slowed up my escape, and, naturally, as I lay there with my head bleeding, it was Marie who came to my aid. For the record, I got a small cut and a massive dose of humiliation, and (once she made sure I was alright) I was a sitting duck for Marie's organizational zeal. This, I thought, as I baked 324 cupcakes at three in the morning, was a mistake. Clearly I still need to avoid Marie (or learn to say no to her, but frankly the running has better odds); it's just that the next time I need to, I will have my getaway route plotted like the theme from *Mission: Impossible* should be playing while I'm at it.

These mistakes at least make sense to me—and that sense is almost immediate. I can feel the enormity of what I've done wrong sweeping over me as the house fills with smoke or the PTA lady looms over me as I lie bleeding in the grass. There's a clear lesson, something I'm supposed to learn, and that makes me feel better. What I hate is when mistakes fall upon mistakes, which heap over errors, which lie atop missteps and are crowned in stupidity resulting from a failure to think, even when reminded to do so, ever so gently—like with a low-hanging branch or 324 cupcakes. Every once in a while, this is how knitting goes for me, and this is how it went, starting one Monday night, when I decided to knit a lace shawl from lovely, proper instructions written by the very experienced Nancy Bush, and ended up Wednesday night with nothing but a reminder that you can have the best directions in the world, but if you won't read them, you're probably going to live through the knitting equivalent of running into a tree . . . over and over and over.

MONDAY AFTERNOON: I cheerfully begin my shawl, casting on hundreds of stitches, and then read the part where the pattern clearly states that the cast on should be accomplished with the yarn held double. I rip it out.

MONDAY NIGHT: I cast on hundreds of stitches again, this time with the yarn held double. Encouraged, I start the first chart, knit competently along for a while, and then realize that I should have stopped knitting with the doubled yarn, like the pattern clearly states. I rip it out.

TUESDAY MORNING: I cast on hundreds of stitches with the yarn held double, drop the extra yarn and knit a row, and then realize I should have started the chart like the pattern clearly states. I rip it out.

TUESDAY AFTERNOON: I cast on hundreds of stitches with the yarn held double, drop the extra yarn and start the chart, then realize that I have not cast on the number of stitches clearly stated in the pattern but have actually transposed the numbers. I have 313, not 331. I rip it out.

TUESDAY NIGHT: I cast on hundreds of stitches with the yarn held double, drop the extra yarn and start the chart, then realize that although I have been aiming for 331 stitches, I have failed counting 101, and have a number that is not 331, nor 313, nor any number that makes sense at all. I rip it out.

TUESDAY NIGHT STILL: After a bloody strong drink to help me get over the bitterness that something I do for fun is kicking the crap out of me, I cast on hundreds of stitches with the yarn held double, drop the extra yarn and start the chart, then realize that I have ripped and reused this yarn so many times that it totally looks like the dog's breakfast and is crap. I rip it out and toss the mangled yarn.

TUESDAY NIGHT STILL: I cast on hundreds of stitches with the yarn held double, drop the extra yarn like I'm supposed to, smugly start the chart (which I have knit so many times now that it is likely burned into my memory for all time, likely replacing useful memory storage like where I put my keys), and knit several rows (also smugly, for I have finally got this thing licked) only to realize, when I have thousands of stitches knit, that I am absolutely knitting on the wrong needles and have nothing even vaguely resembling gauge (which wouldn't matter because, damn it, how does a shawl not fit?), but understand that knitting yarn loosely takes more yarn and I don't have an unlimited amount of yarn and that's another good reason to get gauge and—damn it—I rip it out and go to bed.

WEDNESDAY MORNING: I fetch up smaller needles. I cast on hundreds of stitches. I recount many times and feel sure that I have 331. I place markers every 50 stitches to ensure that I have 331. I count to 50 six times and 31 once. I confirm with a calculator that this is actually 331. I recount to ensure that I have not made a mistake. Then I rip it all out because I forgot to hold the yarn double.

WEDNESDAY AFTERNOON: Using the smaller needles, I cast on 331 stitches with the yarn held double, placing markers every 50 stitches six times and use the calculator and check a whole bunch of times, drop the extra yarn and cut it so that I can't forget that the next row is the yarn alone, and feel really, really good about the idea that I have actually managed not to knit like an idiot for, maybe, fifteen whole minutes in a row. I celebrate by declaring it beer o'clock, work for a while, and then go to the corner store and photocopy the charts so that I can mark them up within an inch of their lives and maybe prevent further knit trauma, and leave for Knit Night.

WEDNESDAY EVENING: I knit the first row of the chart and complain a little bit to the Knit Night ladies that this row is really hard because the chart starts right away, right after the cast on, and that makes double decreases sort of rough and is a little unusual. I persevere, however, and do not complain (much) until I get to the end of the row and have the wrong number of stitches left over. I curse violently, and recount the stitches to make sure that I have the right number. I do. That means I made a mistake with the chart, and I carefully scrutinize that chart, which is clearly marked "Right Side" for about ten minutes before the sick realization comes over me that if there is a "right side" there is likely a "left side" and I slowly, as in a horror movie, rifle my papers until I discover the thing. The world jiggles a little as I realize that I am going to have to rip the stitches back out. The Knit Night crowd asks me what's wrong and I say I don't want to talk about it . . . but then I do. At length.

I start trying to tink back the stitches to avoid another rip, which I fear might take the will to knit right with it. After dropping several stitches back into the cast-on edge, generally screwing up and knitting like I am stunned as a bat, I cram the whole thing into my bag, fish out sock yarn, and knit some nice, quiet 2×2 rib, just to remember I'm okay at this.

WEDNESDAY NIGHT (BACK AT HOME): I rip the whole thing out, perhaps aggressively, and with some language unbecoming to a knitter of my age and station. I toss the now mangled yarn and try again. I cast on 331 stitches (quadruple checking) with the yarn held double. I drop the extra yarn and start the "right side" of the chart. I curse and swear about having to start the chart right after the cast on without even a row of knit to make things nice and when I am halfway across, it occurs to me that this might be a good time to double-check Nancy's instructions, and that's when I see it: "knit two rows" before you start the chart. Clear as day. Right there. Totally right there. Missed it because I was working from the photocopies and didn't look at the book. Rookie mistake. Bonehead mistake. Totally lame mistake. I rip it out, maybe weep a few hot tears of fury, try really hard to remember if I even like knitting, and start over.

This time, all goes well. I cast on 331, yarn double. I knit two rows, yarn single. I start the "right side" of the chart, mark the center stitch, and knit the "left side" of the chart. I even get the right side on the right and the left side on the left. All goes well until I get to the end of the row and have stitches left over, but do have 331 stitches, which would be grand except there were decreases and it should be less. But I have no idea where it went wrong and I don't know if I even care and for a terrible moment there in the middle of the night I may have thought about the fact that I have Nancy Bush's phone number and maybe I might just hold her personally accountable for my pain, even though it isn't her fault at all and that's not why she gave me her number, and that if I have to rip this out again, which I totally do, because the four rows (4) that I have knit are arse, I am going to hurt someone (and seriously, how hard can this be?). Then I toss it in a basket, watch a rerun of *Law & Order*, drink two glasses of wine, think about chewing the yarn into little bits, and go the hell to bed.

I am now knitting a garter stitch scarf in an attempt to protect my sanity and the lives of those around me.

Fear me.

ODE TO SLOW

$\mathcal{I}$ am a free-range knitter. I knit everywhere I go and almost all the time, and this lands me and my yarn in public pretty often, doing our thing. If you knit around regular people, you'll notice sooner or later that they want to talk about it. (The same is true, by the way, if they see your stash. Unless you'd like to take a stab at explaining that you don't belong on an episode of *Hoarders,* maybe keep your stash out of view as much as you can.) It turns out that despite my best efforts, knitting and knitters out in the open are still infrequent occurrences in most of the Western world, and it's interesting to watch people try to make sense of this event. Some people try to ignore it but fail, stealing odd glances over their books on the bus, watching intently while pretending they're not, but other, bolder people will begin a conversation about it. (Let us forget, just for now, about the third group, who want to talk about your knitting but not with you. They'll sit feet away from you and have a conversation about you and your knitting as though you were deaf. "Hey, Martha, look at that lady there. See that?

She's knitting, I think. That's peculiar, isn't it? She seems sort of odd . . .")

The people who would like to discuss it with you, they aren't always sure how to start, and so they invariably ask first, just to be sure, "Are you knitting?" (Every once in a while on a cranky day when I'd rather not discuss my behavior with a stranger or be an ambassador for knitting, I am tempted to say, "Nope. Not knitting" while continuing to do so. I feel sure it would put a stop to the whole business, though it's untested.) Generally, I answer that yes, I am indeed knitting, and when they ask what, I tell them it's a sock (my out-of-home knitting of choice) and then they all watch for a bit. This reaction is pretty universal. I used to think that they were just interested, but it turns out that the staring and silence is really a symptom of someone who's suddenly rather busy adjusting their world view to a place where socks can be made, not just bought. Once they've made this shift, they ask one of two questions. If they contain knitter-potential, usually they ask if it's hard to do. (This is because they're already thinking about doing it themselves.) If the knit-force is not with them, usually the next question is, "How long does it take to make a pair of socks?" It's not an unreasonable question, since even moving at a good clip it's pretty obvious that socks aren't churned out in less than an hour. Knitting, even fast knitting, is still slow, and so I tell them the truth. A pair of socks takes me fourteen to twenty hours of knitting, depending. At this point, most normal people recoil in horror, tell me how unreasonable that is, and silently renew their inner commitment to getting socks the normal way, from the store.

I am not unsympathetic to them. If you really think about it, knitting is absolutely a ridiculous way to get clothes. Before you all get out the pitchforks, let's be honest. A pair of socks from the store cost almost nothing, comparatively. They are cheap in terms of both time and money. Sure, homemade socks are infinitely better, but most folks haven't experienced the supreme wonder that is a pair of perfectly fitting socks; They've been dodging along happily with their discount store socks forever, and no harm has come to them, and because there's nothing wrong with the logic of our detractors, it can be hard to convince them that knitting makes sense. Most of us could get good, serviceable clothes that you can wear in public without shame for next to nothing, again comparatively speaking. Every store has swathes of socks for a few dollars, and whole racks of sweaters that you can pick from, and for less than thirty bucks and an hour of your time, you can be standing in a sweater that fits and doesn't need the ends woven in. In the face of that, how do we defend what we're doing? The yarn for a sweater alone would be more than $30 a lot of the time—hell, I've knit thirty-dollar socks and forty-dollar mittens. They can have socks for next to no money and in no time, but ours are pricey on all accounts, and they can't find a way to relate it to other things that maybe they themselves do—or have seen done—and understand.

Think of the painting on the ceiling of the Sistine Chapel— the pope's personal chapel. Do you have any idea how long Michelangelo stood with his neck twisted up on a freaking scaffold to come up with that? Four years. Four years to have a ceiling painted. It's got more than 300 figures and it's widely regarded as one of the most remarkable works of art within the entire realm of human expression. It isn't just a painted ceiling of 5,000 square feet; it's 5,000 square feet of frescoes—paintings done on wet plaster one little bit at a time—largely by one guy. Just consider that. Did anyone say to Michelangelo, "Hey, Dude, aren't you getting a crick in your neck from painting that ceiling for so long? Isn't this sort of ridiculous, slow, and expensive?" Did anyone take him aside and say, "Mike, baby, wouldn't it make more sense to just paint the ceiling white with a big old roller and put the paintings on the walls like everybody else?" Nope. They didn't, and even in retrospect nobody thinks it was a crazy undertaking. In fact the Vatican spent twelve years and many millions of dollars restoring the whole she-bang a while ago. Obviously, even though it was technically a stupid way to paint a ceiling (if we're following the sock rule), it's got a value that makes sense to us, enough sense to value and invest in it. We get that, and we get other aspects of it too.

Take food. Almost everyone understands that there's a value in taking the time and money to prepare a beautiful dinner for a family or guests. Almost nobody thinks that you're being ridiculous if you spend a whole day in the kitchen making something gorgeous, almost nobody is going to ask you why you're bothering, and almost nobody will suggest that you're entirely off your rocker for not picking up boxed macaroni and cheese and winging it at the lot of your guests. (I keep saying "almost" because I want to leave room for the possibility that one terrible day I'm going to be reduced to serving just that, likely as a result of knitting too much.) Almost nobody is going to suggest that the weird powdered cheese is a better option than, well, just about anything you could give to your guests . . . and maybe that's where we start helping them understand how knitting your clothes really is something that makes sense.

That powdered cheese and stale macaroni might be what gets you through a particularly scrappy Tuesday when you're really only coming up with dinner because you're too pretty for prison, and that's where they send parents who don't provide children with food, but you still understand the value of that slow, special meal you could be making. We all understand that it's cheaper and easier to grab takeaway on the way home and fling it at the ravening hordes, but nobody uses that as a reason why you're not serving up McDonald's at Thanksgiving. Special things, like homemade bread and soup, or a cake you made yourself, are slower. They take a long time, and they cost extra money, energy, and effort, but it's well understood that your time and money are really that secret ingredient that your mum used to say that she was adding—the one she called love. The value of what you put into making something is transferred to that thing, and it becomes valuable just by containing it. Why knit socks? Why not serve sandwiches at weddings?

All of this means something—something good—about investing and going slowly, and putting your time and money into your efforts to show you care, and that is something that should reassure the slower knitters among us. The longer it takes you to make something, the more valuable it is.

ONCE UPON A TIME

Once upon a time there was a very nice knitter who lived in a tiny two-story house with a lot of yarn, a chronically late husband, and some untidy teenagers. This may sound a lot like the beginning of a fairy tale, but this knitter was keenly aware that she was not a princess because a princess would have had way less laundry and way more of a castle, which is really not what you call a house with only two closets, but I digress.

Despite the wee house and the very minor failings of her family (and sadly, herself) the knitter still thought that mostly she was living something absolutely close enough to a fairy tale, because even though the place seemed to be seriously short of dusting elves or pastel birds that hung up the laundry for her, things were really pretty good. Nobody in the house was ever hungry; though the house was tiny, it was warm and safe; and the knitter did have all the yarn she could ever need for her whole life . . . although she doesn't really like to talk about that, because it makes her family ask questions about why it is that she keeps buying yarn, so for the purposes of moving the story along, let's gloss over that little detail.

One fine day when the sun was shining and the knitter was doing what she did best, which would be sitting around working on a sweater while planning to play dumb when the family discovered they were out of bread, as well as contemplating what other women did with their hair that made it look so much better than hers, she began to run into trouble. As our intrepid knitter began the armhole shaping with a predictable bit of casting off to begin the hole, she turned the page to the next instruction, and there it began. The next instruction was something like "cast on a few and then increase a whole whack," and really, any way our knitter tried to slice it, that's not how armholes go. For there to be a hole, there needs to be fewer stitches, we're all pretty sure of that, but knitting can be odd as fish, and every knitter has met a pattern that makes no sense but still makes a sweater, so this knitter, despite being really pretty experienced and clever at this business, tried hard to make the instructions work.

Some time later, the air thick with expletives and generally unladylike language, the knitter was casually gnawing on the edge of her counter to relieve a little stress while she tried to figure out what could be wrong. Not only didn't the instructions work, they didn't even occur over the right number of stitches, and try as she might, the knitter couldn't comply with them—

but she was still committed to trying. She wasn't giving up, partly because she doesn't like to think of herself as a quitter or someone who can have her spirit broken by an inanimate object like yarn, and partly because of the nature of knitting errors themselves. Knitting errors are sneaky. They lurk in corners waiting for a knitter to let down her guard, and then they insinuate themselves into the work. It's not like a mistake in tennis where the ball sails past you and you're instantly aware that you're wrong about where the ball is in space and time. It's more like a mistake in baking, where a cake might simply fail to rise while it's in the oven. The mistake isn't clear, glaring, and immediate. It's sneaky and underhanded and reveals itself slowly while you stand around hoping against hope that it still might come together.

Knitting mistakes being what they are, and this knitter, being intimately acquainted with that truth, had done what almost all experienced knitters do when they find a mistake. She had carefully examined the most recently row knit; she had determined that it didn't have the right number of stitches to make the next row work; she had decided that it was therefore wrong; and then (having been shafted by something like this before, in a way that was absolutely memorable) she had gone to her trusty box of all-knowing (a laptop connected to the Internet) and had asked that box if there were any corrections to the pattern. There were not, and so, heaving a sigh of enormous regret, the knitter ripped back a row of her work, and checked there for the offending error that was the source of the armhole's bizarre nature.

Sadly, so sadly, that row didn't have the right number of stitches either, and so the knitter went back another row, cursing violently, and another, cursing violently *and* creatively, and so on, ripping back row after row, checking the pattern a million times, and recounting a million times, and trying really, really hard to understand how she could begin with the right number, follow the instructions for increasing and decreasing the right way, and still end up with the wrong number, and then the phone rang.

Now in most fairy tales, this would be the moment where the fairy godmother showed up. In a flurry of wings and sparkles, a kindly fairy godknitter would descend upon our poor knitter and not only wave a magic wand and sort this sweater out, but have the leftover sock yarn sorted in a way that made it seem usable and reasonable, instead of a weirdly obsessive collection that nobody in their right mind would be keeping. (Having given it a great deal of thought, I'm also convinced that she would be wearing a handknit gown with a beaded entrelac bodice. It's the only possible thing that could give her the credibility she needed to be taken seriously as a reliable rescuer of knitters.) We've already determined, however, that this is not a real fairy tale, and that this wasn't a real princess (you could tell by the frazzled expression and ruined demeanor—princesses never have ruined demeanors) and so the person on the other end wasn't a fairy godmother but a knitting friend of our hapless knitter, which was mostly the next best thing. This friend was used to knitting ruining demeanors and being the source of foul language, and was immediately sucked into solving the problem. She asked all the relevant questions: Were the right number cast on? (They were.) Had the knitter stopped knitting her size and accidentally taken up with another? (She had not.) Had she checked for errata to the pattern? Consulted the Internet? Considered that the yarn was faulty? (When all else fails, blame the unlikely.)

When they had exhausted the obvious, our knitter threw a massive fit, slammed the teakettle around for a bit, and had a bit of a cry, and then her friend had a clever thought. "Hold on," she said. "Let me get my copy of that pattern; we'll walk through it together." So it came to pass that the knitters began to scour the pattern, line by line, looking for where the whole thing had come off the rails. "See that?" asked our knitter. "Right there at the bottom of that page. Cast off twelve stitches. That makes sense. I did that. Sixty four is what I had, then I cast off twelve which should give me fifty-two, which I have . . ." (They paused there to get a calculator. That may seem like simple math, but a failure of simple math could have been the root of all evil here, and it would have been ridiculous not to double check that it hadn't changed.) "Now look here!" exclaimed our knitter. "It ends there, you turn the page, and everything becomes madness. Suddenly there are supposed to be seventy stitches, and that's not right, unless I was supposed to cast on twelve instead of cast off twelve . . . but that still doesn't come out right . . . and then look here!" She paused to stab the offending sentence hard with her finger, mostly because it was hard not to be angry when there were the ruins of a sweater on the table with its yarn pulled out like innards at a goring. "Here you're to cast some on and then begin increasing again. I don't see how that's going to make an armhole unless I'm trying to put wings on it!" She was enraged to gasping by now and shoved both the book and the yarn violently away from her. "That's it!" she screeched, sort of aware that she was starting to sound like a harpie, but depending on her friend to understand. "I don't get it. I hate this book. I hate this sweater, the yarn is stupid too, and I can't believe that anyone even allowed something like this to be published. You'd think they'd be more careful. This page is fine and then you turn it and it's like the bloody editor nipped off and got blasted. This is my time they're playing with, and for an instruction to be so reprehensibly wrong is just . . . well, it's reprehensible. Maybe it's a joke or even on purpose. The lot of them are sitting around the yarn company right now, laughing until they can hardly breathe, just thinking about me losing my mind. I bet that's it. I should write a letter. I should . . ."

Here, having patiently been waiting for an opening, and seeing that one was not forthcoming, the knitter's friend gently interjected, "Steph?" (It is a complete coincidence that the knitter has the same name I do.) "Steph? I'm not seeing what you're seeing. I see that page seven is fine . . . then I turn the page and page eight makes sense, too . . ."

It was at this moment that all the good sense and ability to double check and problem solve was restored to our fair knitter, and, with a sinking feeling, she looked at her page numbers. Page seven . . . flip . . . there it was. Page ten. For one horrible moment she wondered if her book was faulty and it was still someone else's fault, and she took a deep breath, surveying the carnage of the sweater and the afternoon in front of her, and then she rubbed the pages a little between her fingers . . . and the two pages that had been stuck together fell apart without so much as a whisper of a sound.

The silence was eerie, and the knitter could tell that her friend was sore afraid. "Never mind," said she, and ever so gently hung up the phone, and went to lie in the road.

THE FAT SWEATER

*I*f there was some weird game show where contestants had to match people to their wardrobes, I think that I would be a really easy one, as long as we stuck to my store-bought clothes. I am a sensible woman who doesn't own lipstick, nail polish, or high heels, and I pride myself on my practical and reasonable approach to my wardrobe. I like plain, simple clothes for a whole bunch of reasons. I like plain clothes because I'm sort of shy and I don't like to stand out and because I am physically modest and don't care for anything flashy or low cut. Also, I think I missed the day at school when they explained how to put together an outfit. So, in a desperate attempt to make sure that I don't put together the wrong things, I've decided to err on the side of caution. Plain black pants go with any plain top, plain shirts go with jeans every time, and plain tops and plain pants can always go together, especially if they are the same color. This does make me look like I'm wearing a uniform a lot of the time, but I figure that it's better for people to say, "Hey, Steph? Did you know that when you wear a brown top and brown pants you sort of look like a dishwasher repair guy?" than, "Hey, Steph? There's no easy way to say this. You know that seizure that Marie had? It turns out that the doctors think it was caused by the way your shirt and pants clashed." I have fashionable teenaged daughters, and I can't count the number of times that I've gone to them with an outfit that I think is pretty good, only to have them tell me that it's too much or not enough or that I'm dressed like a dishwasher repairman or that they are starting to see the flashing lights that they think indicate that the combination of my skirt, blouse, and jacket are giving them a wee bit of brain damage. I can always tell that I've misstepped when I ask them if I look okay and they say, "It depends. Are you leaving the house?"

I never managed to learn all the fashion rules that other people seemed to know, and my own mother is still trying to get me to care about them even now, telling me things like women as short as I am shouldn't wear long skirts because it only makes them look shorter, or that I would look taller if I didn't "chop myself in half" by wearing different colors on my top and bottom. This has only ever confused the hell out of me, because she also says I look too plain when I wear the same color on the top and bottom. I think I'm still five foot one no matter what I wear, and there's likely no disguising that.

Finally, I love plain clothes because, as a knitter, I'm looking for things that are a plain canvas for my knitwear. A fancy lace shawl is more impressive over a plain black shirt than it is over a patterned blouse that's going to steal some of the show. What's in my closet might be a train wreck, but it's no accident. Here is what I believe about the store-bought things that I own.

I believe that I do not have many clothes.

I believe that I only keep clothes that I wear often and that fit me.

I believe that I don't have many clothes that don't make sense, or that I will never have occasion to wear.

I believe that the things that I have are mostly plain, functional, comfortable, useful garments that reflect my personality.

If you knew that about me, and if you saw me on that game show with my store-bought clothes on a wardrobe rack behind me, you would be able to match us up. You'd win. This is, however, only true as long as you look at the things I have bought from a store. My knitting wardrobe—the things I've made over the years and years I've been knitting—looks like nine knitters (or one with multiple personality disorder) all live here. All of these knitters have a different personal style and are a different height and dress size, and it would be pretty much impossible to nail down their favorite color. Is it blue? Green? The mountain of handknits upstairs tells no tales. It's the opposite of the store-bought clothes. As orderly, boring, and plain as that wardrobe is, that's how much of the knitting wardrobe is eclectic, colorful, and, frankly, downright strange, especially considering my lifestyle. There are Fair Isle sweaters, brightly patterned in colors that look good together, but not together with me. There are enormous pullovers, tiny tanks—it is eclectic, insane, ill-fitting, and adventuresome, but a knitter would understand. A knitter would take one look at that collection of handknits, and rather than think that I was attempting to assemble my own personal Goodwill shop, I think they'd recognize a pattern. A lot of it is there because I wanted to try the knitting. A lot of the stuff is different sizes not because my weight fluctuates by sixty pounds eight times a year, but because gauge is a fickle mistress and sometimes I finish things that aren't working because, darn it, the knitting is good.

There is one sweater in particular that I call The Fat Sweater. It is brightly colored, roughly the size of a barge, and, were I to put it on, I would drown in it. There is so much yarn in that sweater that if I happened to be caught in the rain while I was wearing it, I would be driven to my knees by the weight. The Fat Sweater meets none of the personal wardrobe rules I think I live by. It does not fit; it doesn't make sense; and it is as far from plain, functional, and comfortable as is wearing a sequined tube top to a parent teacher meeting. I do, however, wear it sometimes. It is fine knitting, brilliantly done, and as a freestanding object, I'm as proud of it as I would be if it were a painting. To my knitterly way of thinking, why wouldn't I wear it? (The answer, of course, is because it doesn't fit, doesn't flatter, is sixteen years old, knit in all the colors of the early '80s, and it makes me look like I steal handknits from the closet of a knitter of preternatural size.)

Alongside The Fat Sweater is an extremely elegant wrap knit of a novelty yarn. It is the exact opposite of everything I have ever bought. It is, in fact, everything that this tree-hugging, ultra-hippy, vegetarian knitter abhors, and yet I love it with a passion that knows no bounds. It is 100 percent unnatural fibers, it sparkles, it was a serious pain in the arse to knit, and it was expensive. It is the anti-Steph. Despite all of this, I have knit it, I have kept it, and I love it. I knit it because I have a mental image of me in the wrap. I'm wearing it with a clingy little black dress, and a pair of tiny little strappy heels. I look inexplicably tall. My hair is doing a fabulous Sarah Jessica Parker thing, and I am at a cocktail party, delicately holding a martini in one hand and a black beaded handbag in the other. I'm discussing politics without getting angry, and I make several good points, and my lipstick is exactly the right color, and at this party in my mind, all the other women want to be me as I glide along, making conversation that's as sparkly as my wrap, and all of that is possible only because I knit it.

The reality is that when I put this wrap on, I am wearing it to the grocery store over my jeans with a pair of Birkenstocks.

I don't own a little black dress, nor strappy little heels, and the last party I went to had fourteen nine-year-olds and a cake in the shape of a Barbie. I beat my hair back with four kinds of product to suppress its will to ever spring forth into "country singer hair," and I need at least thirty minutes' notice to come up with any lipstick, never mind one the right color. When other women see me, they don't wish to be me. They generally thank their lucky stars that they have escaped my fashion destiny and incredible ability to overlook the fact that my cardigan is misbuttoned.

Still, despite all that, I have that wrap draped over a hanger in my closet, right next to The Fat Sweater. This means something, doesn't it? It could mean that I'm a lunatic who is so out of touch with reality that I've got a sparkly wrap for no reason, but I choose to believe that it means that I'm one step closer to being able to say, "One moment, I'll be right with you," when Pierce Brosnan comes to the door to take me to a James Bond-esque cocktail party, with The Fat Sweater tossed in the backseat in case we need a tent.

The truth is that knitters have two wardrobes: the one that is their clothes, and the one that is the product of dreams, skill, hope, or possibly a 50 percent off yarn sale. We make no sense in the outside world, but in our world, we are brilliant. If you see a knitter in a fat sweater, or a garment that is otherwise ill fitting, sparkly, or with gratuitous cables, lace, or color, don't be too hard on them. We aren't wearing it because of how it makes us look. We're wearing it because we made it, and because we're not regular people, we're knitters, and that means that we believe that the beauty of what we have made will be miraculously transferred to us. Somehow.

PRODUCTIVE

*R*ecently I was having a beer with my friend Peter, who is one of those rare human beings who enjoys beating knowledge into children: He's an elementary school teacher, and we were talking about problem solving and children. (Not necessarily that children are problems that need solving, but teaching children to solve problems.) He says that most people problem solve reproductively, which is to say that they think about the way they have done things before, and do it that way again. With a little practice, my teacher friend claims that all of us can be taught to think productively instead, which means that we come up with as many solutions as we can, and consider them all before we charge off with our tried and true answer. He drew a diagram for me, filling in a chunk of graph paper with a few Xs and many Os, and then asked. "How many Os?"

Thinking reproductively, I followed a rule I've known my whole life. If you would like to know how many of something there are, you should count them. It's a system that has served me well, so ticking across the rows, I began to count up the

Os. My friend stopped me, and pointed out that there were far, far more Os than Xs. "Wouldn't it be faster," he proposed, "to count the squares in the height and width, multiply those two numbers to get a total, then count the few Xs and subtract them from the total, rather than spend all the time counting the many, many Os?" I stared at the diagram as Peter went on. "Children need to learn this—to think beyond the first answer, to stop and ask, 'Is this the fastest way to do something, or the smartest?' That's productive thinking. The job of a teacher is to give kids a hundred skills so that they're free to apply their own creativity, and that's what happens when we teach them to think productively." I nodded sagely, trying hard to acknowledge what he was saying while simultaneously trying not to look like someone who hadn't just failed a thinking test over a beer. "This," Peter said (likely while trying to forget that his friend had just failed a thinking test over a beer), "is the difference between genius and regular folk." He paused for effect. "Genius looks for the other ways to think about things, the other ways to solve a problem, the other ways to look at the problem entirely. It's not necessarily about having a high IQ. It's about knowing the right way to think about things, and then thinking a lot." He took a sip of his drink and stared off into the night for a minute. "If we could teach all kids to think like this . . . Give them a bunch of skills, then show them how to use them . . ." Peter broke off and stared again, no doubt imagining his acceptance speech when he won an award for being the best teacher in the world for changing it all. Me, I'm a mother of the kids he's talking about turning into geniuses. Essentially he was talking about creating an army of child brainiacs, and there's no mother on Earth who can't look into that future and imagine what it would be like if all the kids were smarter than all the parents. We've barely got the upper hand as it is—hell, there are days when I'm arguing with my daughters and I regret having taken prenatal vitamins.

On the way home on the bus, I thought about what he had said. If people had lots of skills, and could be taught to think this way, would they be geniuses too? Is it too late for grown-ups? Are we doomed to be intellectually dwarfed by our children? While I don't think I'm a genius, I like to think I'm pretty clever. I knit, I write books, I dress myself—even Peter must think I've got enough sense to understand what he's saying, or he wouldn't have given me the opportunity to fail his test. I even think of myself as a productive, creative thinker. I like to think that knitting trains you for it. The easiest, clearest way to solve a problem in knitting is to rip back your work and do it again. If you make a mistake, that's what we all think to do first. Well, truthfully, usually we think something foul right before that, but then we think of ripping back. It's the knitting equivalent of counting if you want to know how many of something there is. It's obvious, it works every time, and it will absolutely solve your problem. If you make a knitting mistake, and you rip back and re-knit, that problem will cease to exist. The error is gone. (This assumes, of course, that you don't immediately knit the same mistake in again, but that's another sort of learning that we can talk about another day.) That's the simple, reproductive answer, but as knitters, we're pretty likely to reject it . . . aren't we?

When I see a mistake in my work, even though I know it might involve ripping back, my first thought is about how to get out of ripping. Ripping my work out is a painful, destructive process. It's unknitting, watching my time unravel right in front of me. Though I know it's the best answer sometimes, I always look for the wiggle room. I've said to other people lots of times that we all shouldn't mind ripping and redoing work—I mean, it's more knitting, and we like knitting. The truth is, the minute I see the mistake, the bargaining begins. Can I live with the mistake? Is it that bad? Will other people notice? Since I channel all of the perfectionist tendencies I have into knitting so that I can be married and loved, I always assume that if I notice, then someone else will too . . . or more truthfully, I'll notice, and that means I'll never love or wear this piece of knitting because who could possibly go out in public with a mistake on their knitting that makes them look like a moron? (Despite the fact that I never, ever notice the mistakes on others' knitting, I remain convinced somehow that those same people will point and laugh if they see a mistake on mine.)

Once I confirm that the mistake does indeed need fixing and something must be done, I still look to avoid ripping. Can I fix it on the next pass? Pick up a missed yarn over? Change a knit to a purl? If I can't fix it on the next pass, I'm still not done with the avoidance techniques. I start thinking harder. Can I drop a few stitches down a bunch of rows, fix the mistake, and ladder them back up again? I've done some highly inventive and unreasonable stuff in that department. If a mistake is way back at the beginning, often deconstructing a chunk of the sweater makes a lot more sense than ripping all the finished work. (Sometimes this is only the best solution emotionally, though, not saving me any time, just avoiding the pain of watching it all come undone.) I've sewn over cables to make them appear that they go in the right direction; I've worked duplicate stitch over mistakes in colorwork, erasing all evidence that I momentarily followed a chart as well as a stoned bat with a first-grade education.

It is, I reason, really productive thinking. I'm glad to realize this, really, because I was sort of demoralized by the idea that Peter thought this concept should be taught to children and then I didn't do it. If the definition of productive thinking is that you look at all the possible solutions and settle on the best one, then that's exactly what I do with knitting. That's good news, because it means that when Peter's army of super-smart children swarm the Earth, seeking the upper hand, knitters will stand a chance against them.

LOSING GROUND

A while ago, I made a timing error related to a knitting deadline that was pretty catastrophic. For reasons I won't go into here, but mostly having to do with me being a complete procrastinating idiot, I found myself needing to knit eight socks in eight days. Eight adult-sized, sock-weight socks. I was pretty worried about this as a goal. Every Christmas I try just about the same thing, and it's never really worked, but in keeping with my usual ability to delude myself, I decided that this was going to be difficult but possible. It turned out that it was indeed both.

The biggest barrier to this escapade appeared to be that I couldn't cancel my life. (This is the same thing that goes wrong every Christmas. I always plan on an eighteen-hour knitting day and then get all stunned when people are still expecting me to appear in public or bathe.) I still had to do my job. I still had to cook, care for my family, and fight a daily battle against the laundry. But I did make all the changes I could. First, I managed to convince myself that I was above the human need for sleep, then I rented about seventeen DVDs, and then—without exception and whenever possible—if my hands were free for even a moment, I knit socks. If I was walking, I was knitting. If I was on the phone, I was knitting. If I sat thinking at the computer, I picked up the sock, even if it only meant that I got three stitches done. I knit at red lights. I knit while lecturing the children and frying eggs. I knit continuously. I didn't really have a choice. The deadline I was on for these socks wasn't like the Christmas deadline, where you'd rather have finished socks but you could totally wrap them up on the needles in a pinch—this deadline was firm. It was absolute. There had to be socks if it killed me, and there were. It worked. I admit that toward the end I was a little shattered and given to outbursts of tears or rants about the perils of interrupting me, and it is true that my husband still shudders involuntarily when he thinks of it, but with my wool as my witness, there were eight socks in eight days.

While this whole thing was going down, there was just about nobody who thought I was normal. I mean that. Everybody I knew thought I had taken entire leave of my senses. I knit myself stupid for eight days and I think that some of my friends considered an intervention. They definitely regarded me with a critical eye, and there were repeated questions about whether or not it was necessary or normal. I tried pointing out to all of them that it was like being on any sort of deadline for work. It was like having a report due, rolling out new software, or going into labor. I tried to relate it to something they could understand.

Despite this, nothing brought my non-knitting friends around to a supportive position. It's hard, partly because if you don't knit at all than any knitting seems like a lot of knitting, but it may also have been that I was trying to explain the rational nature of my behavior while wearing a dirty bathrobe and explaining that I'd decided to start limiting fluids because the bathroom breaks were wasting precious knitting minutes. The big surprise, though, were my knitting friends, because as much as they saw it as necessary, they clearly still thought the idea of knitting a sock a day was a big slice of crazy pie. Toward the end, when I was alternately knitting, twitching, crying, and insisting it was not a problem, I pointed out to another knitter that it couldn't be that nuts because it was working. I was knitting a sock a day. He pointed out that really the reason everyone thought it was lunatic was because it was lunatic, that it was truly only possible (and barely, at that) because I was, and I quote, "A good knitter."

That compliment felt great, especially in that moment, and I took it to the bank. I left it there, propping up my knitterly self-esteem, until a while later when I was reading a wonderful book called *A History of Hand Knitting*, by Richard Rutt. In the section about the introduction of the stocking frame in the 1600s, one of the first machines of the Industrial Revolution, he wrote that for the first time there was a way to get stockings (a huge commodity at the time, just as socks are now) that weren't hand knit, and he was comparing the performance of that machine to that of a hand knitter. He wrote " . . . it is a mistake to think that the early knitting frame quickly speeded up the bulk production of stockings. A framework knitter working hard might produce ten pairs a week, while a good hand knitter could make six."* There it was. A good hand knitter could make twelve stockings a week. That sentence was significant to me, because right up until I read that, I believed I was a good hand knitter. Apparently the definition has changed.

My first thought was that maybe the definition of a stocking—not knitters—has changed. It didn't seem likely that in a scant four hundred years we'd changed what we were capable of that much. Maybe it was the scope of the work that I didn't understand, not how they got it done. I think of a stocking as a really big sock, a sock so big that it probably was as much knitting as at least the two modern socks I make, but maybe that wasn't true. Maybe "stocking" was being used here to mean "really short, small sock" or maybe they were knitting chunky yarn at a big gauge, so the stockings didn't take so long. Nope. After further research, it turns out that it's as bad as I had hoped it wouldn't be, if not worse. In *Folk Socks*, Nancy Bush writes about an example of the sort of stockings that you'd expect in Scotland in the 1600s. An old grave yielded up a pair of stockings where the legs were about twenty-three inches long, and the feet were eleven inches. That height (mid thigh on me, but I'm short) seems to be near the norm, though some common stockings seemed to stop just below the knee. (Conversely, some of the fancier ones went higher, and it's important when you're thinking about that to remember that socks only get bigger around as they get higher on the leg.) They were knit at seven and one-half stitches to the inch. Seven or eight stitches to the inch is about what I knit my socks at, and while that gauge seems reasonable, it's also only one of the possibilities. The first stocking frame knit at eight stitches to the inch, and I think they would have created that to make the sort of stockings people were most used to seeing, but there are lots of other stockings from that time that were anywhere up to twenty-four stitches to the inch, which makes me just want to weep.

Six pairs of stockings in a week? Twelve stockings? I couldn't let it go. Admittedly, Mr. Rutt is speaking of professional knitters working at it for a living, but seriously, if I lifted all burdens from you for eight hours a day or more and let you work at stocking knitting for a living, would you be producing twelve stockings a week? That's at least the equivalent of you or I hauling off and trying for about twenty socks during a workweek. Assuming a twelve-hour day and a seven-day week, I'd still be gibbering in the corner.

What happened? How did a good hand knitter go from being this stocking machine to being, well, me? What occurred that changed the abilities of all of us so quickly? I know hardly any knitters who could pull off what almost all knitters did four hundred years ago, and that's not really that long ago, not in a human perspective. Worse than that, my life is a walk in the park compared to theirs. I buy most of my clothes; they made them. I turn on the stove, but they had to chop wood, build a fire, and tend it to accomplish the same thing. I have central heat, a washing machine, and electric lights, and they accomplished everything without any of that, and they did it all while keeping an eye on their eight kids, wishing someone would invent reliable birth control, and worrying about what carried the plague.

I can tell you one thing that's changed: skill and the cultural context that it's in. Back when all this stocking knitting was going down, English children as young as four were being taught to knit. By the time that they were seven or eight they were expected to be making stockings in a way that contributed to the family's income, and by the time they were in their teens, they were proper full-fledged hand knitters with ten or twelve years' experience. That's something we mostly don't have here. I hate to be blunt, but a lot of knitters in North America came to the craft late, when their brains were old and it was harder to learn something. Older people learn more slowly and often don't have the same degree of dexterity. (If you don't believe me on that, you should think about how many twelve-year-olds can learn to skateboard in fifteen minutes, and how many forty-year-olds are going to be hospitalized within the same number of minutes.) It's all the same. Languages, skateboarding, how to program a PVR or DVR, or how to text—the kids are faster, and if you learn when you're little and there's room in your brain, then when you're thirty you're a wicked fast knitter. You've been practicing for twenty-five years. That's got to help. We probably lost a lot of our speed when we stopped teaching it to little kids and came up with child labor laws that made it illegal to force them to practice in a profitable way. Life was hard, it was difficult to make ends meet, and knitting stockings was something that you could do whenever your hands weren't busy, just to try and bring in a little extra cash. During the several hundred years that comprised the stocking boom, everyone knit, and, by everyone, I mean even your father. All were beavering away at knitting, and they couldn't conceive of the luxury of our lifestyles, or the idea that you could have hours of idleness in the evening during which you just watched something or leisurely read a book. Free time was something for rich people. Those who weren't rich had one person read out loud while everyone else knit or spun, just to keep the efficiency high.

By contrast, knitting barely has a cultural context for us. It's hard to comprehend how knitting was regarded four hundred years ago in the British Isles. The expectation was that this skill, which we think of as very specific and difficult, was manageable by just about everyone. Our culture has other expectations that are just about the same. Take driving. Driving a car is a really complicated activity. You have to use your hands and your feet, signal your intentions, read the intentions of others, interpret signs, follow all the rules, and do all of it at exactly the right speed. Still, even though it's that hard, we expect that pretty much everyone will be able to do it with a reasonable degree of dexterity. We've built a culture on it. We expect that, even though one of the consequences for screwing up this common cultural skill is death (which is certainly not true of knitting), you'll be able to do it when you're pretty young and stupid.

On the flip side, we've come to think of everything to do with knitting as pretty highly skilled and specific, and even knitters are tripped out by it sometimes. Ever hear a knitter say, "I'm not ready to cable," or "I'm going to do scarves for a while before I do socks. They look too hard." Sure you have. A couple of hundred years ago, that attitude would have been laughable. They would have laughed at a knitter like that just as hard as you would have giggled if you heard that someone who was out there driving around felt like they weren't ready to signal or do the speed limit, so they were just going to drive the highway at a crawl, hoping that people got the feeling that they were going to change lanes sometime before they did. Our expectation is that if you're grown, you'll be able to handle all the complexities of driving, because it's part of making your life work, and they felt the same way about knitting.

Finally, there was what a stocking represented. It was an income, or it was something to keep you warm, and there was no other way to get them. Either you knit them or you bought them, and even once the stocking frame was invented, it was about another two hundred years before machine-made stockings were cheap enough that their production was meaningful to common people. Sure, we've lost ability, we've lost cultural context, and we've lost the sort of difficult lives where if you didn't work continuously you couldn't manage, but aside from all of that, we've lost one other important thing.

Incentive. Back then, there was an incentive to be a competent knitter. It paid off. Being fast and skilled mattered. Now, if you're not competent or fast you don't really have a lot of problems, other than a big stash that you'll never burn through. If you don't get the hang of socks, there are other places to get them, and you can just be a sweater knitter. You don't have to be a good knitter to be a happy knitter, and that wasn't true in the fifteenth and sixteenth centuries. They were fast and they were good because it mattered. I've compared that a lot to the week that I spent knitting like a fiend, trying to do eight socks in eight days, and if it ever happens to me again, and people look at me like I'm crazy, I'm going to say two things. I'm going to ask them if they signal when they drive, and then I'm going to tell them that, far from being a knitting-obsessed maniac headed for some sort of vague incident concerning the men with the huggy coats and a sedative blow dart, historically speaking, I might be a slacker.

*Richard Rutt, *A History of Hand Knitting* (Loveland, Colo.: Interweave Press, 1987) 85.

LANDMINES

$\mathcal{I}$ close the door, saying good-bye to the postie who's just delivered me a package, and it strikes me that he must wonder about me. This family gets a fair number of packages, and sometimes I see this guy three times a week, and it just occurred to me now (I'm pretty quick that way) that even though he comes in the early afternoon, about nine times out of ten I'm sort of unkempt, clutching a half-knit sock and clad in leisure wear when he arrives. (By calling it "leisure wear," I'm trying to make it sound okay that I'm actually wearing old yoga pants and a coffee-stained T-shirt that says "talk nerdy to me" on the front.) He's never asked me what I do, why I'm always here, or how come I so seldom look like I am prepared to go out in public—and now that I think about it, I wish he would. Compared to what he must be imagining about how I spend my days, I'd rather he knew that I am a writer, a knitter, and that somehow, or at least in my life, that combo means that I don't get dressed as often as other people.

I am not now, nor have I ever been, the sort of person who can just leave the house, although I hear tell that most people can. I even watch my friends and family do it, and I see people walking down the street in the morning, all of them getting up, getting dressed, brushing their hair, picking up their bags, and leaving their houses for work, and, while I salute those people, I can't identify with them. I work from home, and I have a tiny office off of my kitchen, and while I occasionally think about what a leg up on the world you would have if you had the sort of job that made you get dressed every day, I don't want one, and truthfully, when I did have one, it didn't help a lot. Mornings would often find me looking for one of my shoes, discovering my blouse was buttoned funny, and spilling coffee on my last pair of clean pants. (Eventually I learned to have my first cup of coffee naked. It worked pretty well.)

My trouble with leaving for work wasn't just about work. I have the same trouble going anywhere. Even trying to leave for a grocery shop I can't find my list, my keys are gone, and even though I've taken great pains to prevent it from happening again, I have nothing to wear that makes me look like a grown-up who can be trusted. (It has been suggested to me that this may be related to my belief that putting on my one bra is really only for special occasions, but I still find it difficult to believe that controlling your breasts is the secret to being taken seriously.) If this is the sort of person you are, with uncontrolled breasts and naturally messy hair, then it turns out that you may be happier working from home, as I am, where the expectations for my appearance, timing, and foundation garments are a little bit lower. It has been awesome for me, because other than the fact that my postie likely thinks I'm chronically depressed, home moves at the speed and with the priorities I can cope with. I work when I like, eat when I like, talk when I like, and do laundry when I like, and frankly, a commute of ten steps without even having to brush your hair is hard to top.

Working from home has its down side, like that the only structure in it comes from me. You need a fair bit of self discipline about getting yourself to work if you're the only one who's going to notice if you get there. Everyone else has to get dressed and organized every day or their bosses will notice, while a lack of reasonable sensibility on my part could mean that if I'm not careful, I can end up hanging out at my desk in my underwear thinking about how great it would be if I could pay the cat to do housework. (Think that over. She's just lying there.)

I accept who I am—it's hard not to once you're in your forties—but I still sometimes wish that I was that other sort of woman: the kind where you can come over anytime and she's got clothes on, or the kind who can put her hands on her purse without a search-and-rescue mission that takes twenty minutes and a minimum of three family members. To stay in the habit and to keep myself from becoming entirely feral and unacceptable to society, I try to go to a regular Knit Night one evening a week. It's on Wednesdays, and I'm pretty attached to it. Despite my natural tendencies to hang out at home, there's not a lot that can happen to make me miss a Knit Night. I don't go if I'm sick, since, even if I feel almost well enough to go, only a sadist gives a fellow mother a cold—especially if her kids are little. I don't go if I'm working (though I really try not to be working those nights), and I don't go if it's a parenting conflict, like parent–teacher night or a school concert, or something else where your kids will end up in therapy explaining how they were completely unsupported because their mother cared more about yarn than she cared about them. (I understand that my kids will probably need therapy someday anyway, simply because I'm their mother. I just want for it not to be about the knitting.) My point is that I really do try to get out to Knit Night, and some weeks when I'm swamped and my goal to be sort of normal fails, it might be the only time I leave the house for social reasons. That means that without Knit Night, I'm essentially having all my interactions with other non-family humans when they sell me produce or cheese, which worries me. I feel like the only thing that keeps me from falling into an abyss where the neighborhood kids talk about me like I'm some vague legend and call me "The wool lady" is making sure I get out there once a week.

In order to rally against my basic nature, I conceive a huge plan—a grand effort where I plan ahead, try not to let things get in my way, and hope it all culminates in walking out the door at 6:00 p.m. on Wednesday evening looking like someone with clean, matching clothes, brushed hair, and subway tokens. In short, I try to leave looking like someone I'm not. (You can imagine the strain.) All day long I think about what I need to take with me, and I make a little pile on the piano. A skein of yarn I promised Andrea, a bit of fiber for Denny, a book I'm lending Rachel, the book I'm returning to Jen . . . my keys (That's a hard one. I'm bucking a genetic trait for key loss) and, of course, my knitting. I put together one of the few outfits I own that doesn't make me look homeless, and I try not to lose touch with my goal. I get my word count written for the day, I get my e-mail caught up, I even make dinner for the family—which I think is very generous, considering that I won't be there to eat it. I start early in the day, I maintain the focus of a sniper, and I watch out for the landmines that can trip me up and ruin the fragile shot I have at making it out of here. It's like planning an escape from a disorganized, low-security prison.

If you think this sounds like a bit much, just know that a multitude of things have gotten in the way of Knit Night, things that I don't think would happen if I worked outside my home. One week I was all pumped and ready to go, and when I went to get dressed it turned out that I didn't have any clean "outside pants" to wear. Personally, I believe that if I had an outside job I would have noticed way before dinnertime that I had no pants on. Another time I made the mistake of answering a work call too close to leaving time, and got totally shafted into four more hours of work, and while I'm sure people are stalked by mobile phone, it's gotta be easier to avoid your office phone if, at some point, you leave the office. I've missed Knit Night because I screwed up transportation, and again, I think that if I was transported out of that house more often due to necessity, I might be better at that part. To get to Knit Night I have to have all my ducks in a row, and while I'd have fewer ducks to shuffle if I was already dressed, up, out, and organized, there's a cluster of landmines that are a big problem for me—and would be no matter what my job was like. I speak now, naturally, of my children.

The young women who are my daughters are a disorganizing force to be reckoned with. Take your eyes off the prize for even a moment and you're going down, and I have had my plans cancelled by every possible teenaged form of emergency. If I'm planning on going to Knit Night, when the girls come home from school, I launch an exhaustive quiz to make sure they aren't going to mess with me. If you're a parent you know what I mean. You're just about to go out the door and the kid announces that somehow they've roped you into having to produce sixty-four cupcakes (with icing) before daybreak. Once they're old enough to be told to make their own damn cupcakes, then it's things like "very long essays" they forgot about until just now, or some sort of unscheduled breakdown involving a teenaged boy who didn't meet expectations. (I actually really resent that. From what my teenaged daughters tell me, teenaged boys haven't changed much since I was a girl and I'm not sure what it says about evolution that they're still the same or that we're still shocked about it.) On a day that I'm planning to leave the house, I inquire about boys and about school, and I also ask about friends, because last week I didn't get to go to Knit Night because that skanky Allison in French class told one of my girls she thinks that the reason Daniel isn't talking to her is because her hair isn't nice, and it took me forty minutes to get the teen to stop sobbing and then wrestle the hair products from her hands. (I considered leaving anyway, but she was locked in the only bathroom.)

This Knit Night, though, this time I have it nailed. I am aware of all the landmines before me, I am determined to buck my nature, and I have been working since early this morning to nail an absolute on-time departure. My outside pants are not only clean, but they are ironed, and to protect them from my preternatural gift for pouring coffee in my lap, I am working in my underpants until the last minute. I have been assembling the things I need to take with me all day, following a complex system of Post-It note reminders all over the house. (The final Post-It is on the door and says, "Don't leave without the pile of stuff.") I have prepared a pot of soup and bought bread so that the family has something to eat and I can shrug off the maternal guilt that can wash over me when a clutch of people who are all capable of making their own dinner stand there staring at me as I put on my shoes, as though I am abandoning them in the desert and taking the only water with me. I have found my keys and placed them in the pocket of my pants upstairs, along with a subway token and my bike lock key. (I am covering all my bases.) I've caught up on work, and now that it's getting close to the end of the day I've begun to practice saying, "Sorry, I'm just on my way out. Can we do this first thing tomorrow?" I've said this in my head so many times that I'm starting to think that if the phone rings, I might actually say it. I close my e-mail, reminding myself that since I am going out, there's no point in looking at it until the morning; and in a minute, when the family starts to come home, I'll start checking in with them because after managing to pull off an escape plan this neatly, there's no way that I'm missing Knit Night because a fifteen-year-old girl didn't tell me until three minutes before I'm supposed to leave that she needs three sources to write a review of *Stranger in a Strange Land* and two loaves of bread for the student council lunch, that she's lost her best pink lip gloss that she can't go to school without, and that she's being expelled from science if she doesn't bring $7.85 (exact change required) and a permission form (that she's lost) for a field trip that starts at 7:30 the next morning. I have checked the weather report. I know where my sweater is. My knitting is tidily packed into a bag to take with me, and I've even checked to make sure that I have two needles, the pattern, and a bottle of wine. (If you're only leaving the house once a week, you have to do it right.)

I stand there, looking at all I have wrought, and I feel normal. I'm just like other people, other people who leave the house all the time. I nailed it. I go upstairs to put on my outside pants (it is easier to feel prepared to leave when wearing pants), congratulating myself the whole way. Assuming that when everyone comes in from work, school, and play, I can dodge landmines like parental responsibility, and I'll be out of here. Free as a bird, leaving the house. I'll get to Knit Night and I'll have a glass of wine and I'll knit on the blue sweater I'm making and I'll engage in conversation, and for one glorious evening nobody will know that I'm actually a woman who found cheese in her desk drawer and hasn't worn a matching outfit since last Wednesday. I pull on my pants, proudly pat the subway token and keys in the pocket, and think about how if I really start to get the hang of this, then maybe I could raise the bar—maybe I could start wearing accessories! I see other women wearing accessories and matching outfits, and they look really great and people take them super seriously. For some time, I have thought that accessories were the key to something. I'm not sure what, but there's a big difference between me and the women wearing them. I pop into the bathroom to brush my teeth, and I realize that, really, if this whole leaving on time thing starts to take less effort, then I could think about wearing outfits, and not just clothes, and I could have a hairstyle, not just hair, and I could even wear knitted stuff that matched my coat in the winter! Hell, if I'm going to be this person, a person who plans ahead and organizes stuff and knows where her keys are just like real people . . . I could even wear a hat and mittens that match! I'm giddy. I head downstairs, check the clock, and realize that I have mere moments before the girls arrive. I stir the soup, and when they arrive, I strike like a cobra.

I welcome them home. I ask about their days, but not too much, since I don't really want to know. It's Wednesday; Joe can care today. They need a parent, but it absolutely does not need to be me. I remind them that tonight is Knit Night. Joe comes in, and before he can tell me one of the twenty-six reasons that I shouldn't go, I launch into the whole thing. I show him the soup, the bread, the subway token, and point at my outside pants. When he tries to interrupt me, I tell him I've met my word count, and that I've done most of the e-mails and the rest don't matter, and that some people leave the house every day. They do. They have jobs where the letter carrier doesn't wonder if they're struggling with mental illness and the whole family expects that they're going to leave the house, and those women know where their purses are all the time. Every day. Joe tries again to interject and I cut him off at the knees. I tell him that I want to be one of those people who get dressed every day, and that he shouldn't be arguing with me when I'm just trying to become someone who wears accessories because I think that those women have an easier time at parent–teacher interviews. Joe interrupts again, this time, sort of aggressively.

"Steph, you're a complete lunatic and I love you, and I can tell that you've worked really hard at being all organized, and you can wear accessories if you want to, but I'm really sorry. You're not going to Knit Night tonight."

I stare at him, soup spoon clutched furiously in my hand. What did I miss? I had all the bases covered. School concert? Taxes? Some sort of appointment that isn't on the calendar? Does one of the girls have a fever? Did he see my mother on her way over here? Is it Thanksgiving? Do I have to vote? I sigh, glancing dejectedly at my knitting waiting for me by the door, and wonder if any of my friends are going through this right now. Are all my attempts to be a functioning adult hopeless? Joe watches me, and I can tell that he feels really badly about this. Even though he's occasionally one of the landmines that keeps me from going out the door, I know that he knows that I really want to go to Knit Night, that it's symbolic of getting it together, that when I'm out and about it makes up a little for the way that I feel unpolished and scruffy the rest of the time, no matter how hard I try. Maybe I'm just scruffy and unpolished. Maybe it's never going to be any different. Maybe, just maybe, I should work on loving myself better the way I am. A work-from-home, braless writer with a messy office, a lack of accessories, and a lost purse. Joe rubs my back. I tell him it's okay. I'll try again next week. I'll plan better. Then I buck up a bit, and ask him what it is. What did I miss? What's so important that I can't just walk out the door on a Wednesday night like anyone else?

Joe pulls me in for a hug and puts his arms around me and gives me a squeeze. Then he whispers in my ear the one thing that I can't overcome. "Darling. It's Tuesday."

CRYTOSCOPOPHILIA

$\mathcal{I}$ have a love of odd words. I love finding them out and thinking about how I might have occasion to use them. I delight in imaginary circumstances under which I somehow engineer (at a really posh party with really smart people where I am very thin) a conversation in which I am suddenly able to seamlessly insert a word that I love, completely in context. I imagine the look of respect on their faces as I say that I do know how to play the piano, but I'm not very good, because while I took lessons when I was little, I was a committed misodoctakleidist (a piano student who really hates to practice). Or in a conversation about the supernatural I could say, "Well, Mark, the Bermuda Triangle may seem naufragous, but really, it's not borne out statistically." I would be, you understand, the only person at the party who knew that naufragous means "causing shipwrecks," though nobody would say they didn't know that word because (in the party in my mind) they all want to be like me. (This fantasy may stem from real party episodes where people were glad *not* to be me, like the time I had my skirt tucked into my underpants, but I digress.)

This love of words has yielded up some real treats. For example, I take great joy in knowing (though I have yet to figure out how to work it into conversation) that a ranarium is a frog farm (as a related point, one who eats frogs is batrachophagous). And, likely because I am one of the world's only writers working within the niche field of knitting humor, I have managed to successfully use the word "adoxography," which means "skilled writing about an unimportant subject," in a professional context. My favorite ever, though, the most fulfilling word of all, is "crytoscopophilia." When I first heard it I loved the feeling of it in my mouth—"cry-toe-sco-po-feel-e-ah"—but like most of the really great words I've ever learned, it was the meaning of it that turned out to be what gave it great and odd power.

Crytoscopophilia is the urge to look in people's windows as you pass. The minute I read it I knew it was me. I do that all the time. Out for a walk at night, with the homes that you pass by lit up from the inside, offering little glimpses of the lives inside. It turns out that it's a nearly universal urge, too, since almost everyone who hears it proclaims that they have crytoscopophilia. The few who don't have it think it's creepy, but I defend the practice and point out that crytoscopophilia departs from what those who don't partake in it might call stalking, peeping, or an invasion of privacy in one significant way. The definition is precise. It is the urge to look in windows "as you pass," and that's the relevant part. It stops being crytoscopophilia the minute that you start thinking about standing in someone's rosebushes, or consider fetching a ladder or some night-vision goggles.

I love what I can tell about people's homes just from the momentary vignettes I see. I love the tiny story that is told in that moment as I catch a glimpse of someone putting a book on the shelf, or a couple exchanging words, or a family eating dinner. It sets my mind afire, and I can't help but extrapolate and wonder. What book is going onto the shelf? Was it good? Should I read it? Maybe they were just looking something up? Maybe it's a photo album and this character in my now imagined world is marking the day that they returned from the war and fondly recalling a fallen comrade. Perhaps the couple exchanging words are talking about the bills or maybe they're planning a bank heist in Switzerland. There's just no way to know, and that's the magic. We have no idea what relevance the moment those people are having has to the world, but we are so interested that we actually think that something satisfying and important can be gleaned by knowing that their living room is blue. (Maybe that's just me, but I'm terrifically interested in the decorating habits of my targets.)

Hemingway allegedly wrote one of the world's shortest short stories. It was six words and read, "For sale: baby shoes, never worn." I think about that a lot as I glance in windows and try to figure out what I can gain. It's not about what I can see. As in Hemingway's story, it's about the beauty and intrigue of getting a taste of what I don't know. In that very short story, there is very little stated. You're left to imagine the details. It's precisely that magic that we gain from a crytoscopophilic glance—one tiny nugget of information that sets off a whole stream of imagination. Crytoscopophilia is the magic of inference. What can you tell— or what do you think you can tell—from a narrow flash of insight? Why were the shoes never worn? Was there no baby? Did a baby come but not walk? Is it a tragic story of infertility, or did the family get rich and buy better shoes, relegating these ordinary ones to the sale shelf? There are actually a thousand stories present in that one magnificent phrase, and each one of them is equally possible. Inference is defined as a conclusion reached on the basis of evidence and reasoning, which makes it sound as if it's firm—as in "he inferred from the presence of the snow that it had been snowing," but the magic lies in the other possibilities. With inference, you're working with evidence and reasoning, not facts. Maybe what really happened was that there was snow because a film starring Tom Cruise was made just there, and a snow-making machine the size of Malawi was brought in to transform a hot July street into November for a few short hours. Inference is not just the ability to know what happened based on what you see and know, but the ability to guess at a thousand possibilities.

When looking at ancient languages and the way they move around the globe, linguisticians really have no choice but to use inference to guess at the source of the language. There's nobody to ask and no one wrote down the exact path a language took. There are only clues. For example, if a language has no word for "cow," you can infer that the language comes from a place without cows. A language with no word for artichoke, likely artichokeless. A place with no artichokes and cows? You can put that together and come up with a locale. Linguisticians can tell us that there is no word for knitting in any ancient language on Earth. Not Greek, Roman, Aramaic—nothing. The first appearance of a word for knitting was in the Middle East about 1,000 years ago. In the English-speaking world, nobody draws a picture of it, or includes it in a story, until Shakespeare's time. From that historians can infer that there was no knitting there until that time, and that's a huge thing to know about knitting, and it's derived from inference— little peeks, small pieces—and we all do it. We're convinced it works and that we're truly finding things out.

The trouble is, what have you really found out? Well, knitting really is only about a thousand years old. The information we glean through inference there is reliable and accurate. The trouble with information you get is that it's sometimes accurate, but usually it's not. I personally have had a whole whack of conversations in my life based on nothing more than a little bite like, "Did you hear what he said?" which is a fairly inevitable stop on the way to, "Why do you think he said that?" which leads inexorably to, "I think he likes you." Shockingly, I'm in my forties and have only just now worked out that this system is about as reliable as me walking by a window and deciding that the couple talking inside are planning that Swiss bank heist. It probably means that I'm not hopeless, that I no longer think that the only conclusion a girlfriend should infer should lead her to write what will clearly be her new last name in her notebook seventy times.

Seeing this rampant case of crytoscopophilia in myself, the way that as I get these little bits of information about people around me as I pass, and knowing as I do that this urge is almost universal, it makes me wonder what people infer about me when they look in my windows. Someone passing my house at night and looking in my windows is going to see some stuff a little off the norm. They would likely see me knitting, and from that they might infer that I have a nice hobby. That's a pretty normal thing to think if you see someone knitting. Maybe though, just maybe this person has a dog, and my house is on their evening route and they pass by my house every night.

There's a family on the far corner of my jogging path and I pass by them all the time. Every time I do, there's a man folding laundry and a woman watching TV. After I'd seen them doing the same thing a few times, I started to form opinions—to infer things. I inferred that they're people who like routine. (I can't fault them for that, since I wouldn't know it about them if I didn't have one.) I also inferred that they have a modern relationship—I mean, he's doing the laundry and she's watching TV. Statistically, men in relationships only do 10 percent of the laundry in North America, so as soon as I see that reversal I've decided that he's the best guy on Earth and that their marriage is terrific. Of course, the inference I'm making about this couple is crazy. They might not even be married. They could be roommates, and he's doing his own laundry. It could be that they are married and that she does everything else to do with every single one of the chores, and this is the one thing the jerk ever steps up to the bat for. He could be a neatnik; she could be a slob. She could be allergic to laundry soap, or maybe she has a broken wrist from a nasty fall from a bus, and he's just doing the laundry until it's better. I really don't know—I really don't—but my biases and hopes feed my imagination, and because of my own stuff, I want to believe that they're just so happy together and that they're enjoying the fruits of a noble marriage with a truly gracious and equal division of labor. I can't help it.

I wonder then, about those people who have my house on their route. If they pass by once and see me knitting, it's likely to be interpreted as a moment, a little vignette. It's unlikely that they're going to make a big decision about me or my lifestyle. If they pass my house every day though, they're going to notice that the knitting happens a lot. A whole lot. Regardless of the time of day or night, anyone conducting even the most casual and benign of surveillance is going to come to the conclusion that the amount of time I spend on yarn-related activities is really high. (This is not all my fault, by the way. The amount of time I spend with yarn wouldn't be so bizarre if the rest of the culture I live in wasn't skewing the bell curve by engaging in no yarn activities at all.) Maybe one day, after a while, they would walk past my house, glance in, and, much to their relief, I'm not knitting. "Thank heaven," they'd think, because they really were starting to think that I spent an obsessive amount of time at it. Only then would they notice that, while I'm not knitting . . . I'm sitting at a spinning wheel.

I worry about this. I understand fully and deeply that the ideas that these strangers hold about me can't possibly matter. If someone walks their dog past my house every evening and comes to the conclusion that I'm an obsessive freak with no life, or a social life as barren as the Sahara, there is no possible way that can influence my life, not really. The people who know and love me still will, I'll still have a job, and the roses in the back will still get black spot every summer no matter what I do. Nothing will be better or worse for me if that guy or a multitude of people walking by all decide that I'm boring, old, weird, simple, and likely have a thousand cats that they just can't see. It wouldn't even matter if they all formed a club where on Tuesday nights they all walked by together, casting a crytoscopophilic peek into my window en masse while wearing T-shirts that said, "we glance in the Crazy Knitting Lady's windows together." It wouldn't matter at all. I mean, I wouldn't like it; I would have my own inferences to make about those people, not the least of which would be that they were trapped in a hopeless stereotype about knitters. Nope, it shouldn't matter at all what they think, so the clever part of me is stunned that I really do care what complete strangers might divine from a glance in my window. I want the story they tell themselves to be accurate . . . or at least if it can't be accurate, I'd like for it to be flattering.

I would love for people to walk by, glance in my window, and think two things. First, that I have exquisite taste in home decorating, and second, I'd like for them to see me knitting or spinning and at least come close to inferring the right thing. I'd like them to infer that I'm a fiber artist, intent on using and creating my own raw materials to express myself through a constructive art form that's a thousand years old. Barring that, I'd settle for them at least thinking that what I'm doing is interesting, instead of a sign that time spent with me would likely be as stimulating or appealing as a bowl of cold oatmeal. Realistically I don't expect them to infer it, and I understand that we all come to infer things based on our own biases and theories, and that every single one of us thinks that you can look at what a person does for one second a day and be sure that you know something about them. Hell, the fact that I care what couch you have when I pass by even means that I believe that I can tell something interesting about you from what you own. (This problem is just one of the many reasons that I don't let people open closets in my house.) If I see that you've painted your walls purple with pink stars and hung vivid paintings, obtained a polka-dot couch, and are in the process of hanging chartreuse-striped curtains, then I know I'm not going to think you're shy, even though there are a million reasons (if we remember the rules of inference) why you could be doing that, including that you're colorblind or have lost a hideous bet with your rather cruel, yet creative, cousin Sven.

Crytoscopophilia is the urge to gather information so that we can infer the snot out of something, because most of us think that inference works, even if the truth is that most of us get it pretty wrong a lot of the time. We're simply not neutral enough. We're too biased, and we think we know too much. That one glance I get through your window doesn't explain anything to me about why that man washes your underpants, and it doesn't tell anyone anything about me or the seemingly alarming amount of yarn I have and the shocking quantity of time I spend fiddling with it. It makes me wonder why any of us are crytoscopophilic at all, considering how little of what we gain is of actual use. This is what I'm thinking when I'm out for a walk and I'm glancing in your window, and this is what I'm thinking when you're out for a walk and I see you glancing in mine.

I'm also thinking that I should get curtains that are less sheer, but maybe that's just me.

FAIR TRADE

*W*hen I was twenty, I had an affair with crochet. I didn't want to, because with the exception of Larry King, I'm probably one of the last people you would expect to find taking up with a hook. I am really very monogamous in my relationship with knitting and appear not to have a bi-craftual bone in my body. There's nothing wrong with crochet. I just don't like it, the same way that some people don't like bananas or swimming. (For the record, I don't like bananas either. I feel like there's only a ten-minute window in between when they're too green to eat and when they're dismal, blackened, weeping things on the counter. Bananas take constant monitoring and I can't get behind that. I do like swimming, though.) I've tried to get it together with crochet, but it's never worked out. Nevertheless, one day in 1988, I had an unlikely episode. (Remember that 1988 was also when *Die Hard* came out; Ringo Starr went into rehab; and I had hair the size of a Buick and was wearing a ripped sweatshirt à la *Flashdance*. Anything was possible.) A good friend of mine was getting married, and I dropped off a bunch of craft magazines that had a lot of beautiful knitted things in them at her house and told her to pick her wedding present. I didn't realize it at the time, but, much to my peril, one of the magazines I gave her didn't just have knitting patterns but also some lurking crochet.

A week later the phone rang, she told me that she'd picked the most beautiful knitted tablecloth in the world, and I swung round her place to see what she'd picked. You can imagine what I thought when she opened the magazine and plunked her finger on (and I quote exactly), "The perfect tablecloth," and I leant forward to see what I would be knitting for her. It was crochet. A lace crochet tablecloth. Unbelievable.

I thought about telling her I wouldn't do it. I thought about telling her I couldn't do it. I thought about saying something like, "Oh hell. That's not knitting, choose again." It would have been easy, but before I could get it out of my mouth, she said something like, "this is the most beautiful thing in the world. It is all I have ever wanted, and you're a really fabulous friend for offering to make it for me, because, really, I can't see myself ever loving anything else the way that I love this." (I may be paraphrasing there, but only a little.) What choice did I have? I picked up a really teeny-tiny hook and a totally insane amount of fine crochet cotton, and I vowed to make her a stinking crochet tablecloth.

The only important thing that you need to know about what happened between then and six months later is that, damn it, there was a tablecloth on her wedding day. The less important things that you don't need to know are things like this: Every day that I worked on that tablecloth—many, many days—I thought about things that would be easier and more fun than crocheting a lace tablecloth. Things like running a marathon through Death Valley in August, or shaving the genitals of a wild musk ox—and I am not even exaggerating. Some of the skills I had from knitting were transferable, like the idea of managing string, and the concept of a stitch or following a chart. I had a lot of a leg up over your average beginner, but I'd also decided to go from not crocheting at all to churning out a fine lace tablecloth on a deadline, and that sucks any way you slice it. It was stupid. It took hours, and by hours, I mean days—no, months. My friend wanted this to be an heirloom, and that's what I was going to make her, but nobody could make me enjoy it. I struggled through, I made it work, and, though I haven't seen it lately, my friend has a really nice crochet lace tablecloth, and she had better take good care of it because, seriously, I'm never making another one. It was too hard.

For some crazy reason, probably related to the crochet equivalent of post-traumatic-stress disorder, I haven't thought about that tablecloth for a long time, and I probably would have continued to block it out of living memory if something wild hadn't been said to me a little while ago. I live in a big city, and there's a thriving Chinatown about fifteen minutes from my house. Last year I was down there looking for neat stuff to land in the Christmas stocking of a teenaged girl, and there was a stack of crochet tablecloths, including a big tablecloth—way bigger than the one I made—for about sixty bucks. I didn't think anything of that, but I was with a friend who's a crochet expert, and as I shuddered while I passed the tablecloths, she said something incredible. She just tossed it out there for me to catch. "You know," she said, "that's handmade crochet."

I had a delayed reaction to that statement. I suppose that initially what I thought was that crochet worked like knitting. I don't know if everyone knows, but we all wear a ton of knitting every day. Not just the stuff that makes sense, like socks, sweaters, and hats, but tons of other commonplace items. T-shirts, pantyhose, turtlenecks, sweatpants, bathing suits, underpants—just about everything stretchy is produced by the commercial knitting industry, and I guess that because you can see crochet everywhere like that, I believed there was a big commercial crochet industry. Further to that, the term "handmade" can be confusing. You and me, we would think that "handknitted" means doing what we do, with two sticks, some string, one human, but it turns out that it's perfectly legal for someone to call something "handknitted" if it was made on a knitting machine as long as the knitting machine wasn't automated. If you were running that thing with your hands, if it was powered by you, then that's considered handknitting, and that is what it can say on the label. (As a real handknitter, you will likely find that as offensive as I do, and even now you may be fighting the urge to correct the misnomer with every person that you meet. I'll give you a hint: They will not be as concerned with this injustice as you are.) That is how I thought my friend meant "handmade" crochet. I'd crocheted a tablecloth, and I'm here to tell you that there was no way it would have been sold for sixty bucks. Even once I got good at it . . . sixty bucks?

That $60 represents the whole shebang. There's the markup for the store (usually about 100 percent), the shipping, the packaging, and the manufacture, all coming in under $60. That, I reasoned, wasn't possible if it was actually handmade. A 100 percent markup means that the manufacturer only made $30. Even if you didn't have packaging and shipping costs, and who knows whatever else, even if somehow the person who made the tablecloth got the whole thirty bucks, how could they do it? How's that practical, reasonable, or possible? I reasoned that it just couldn't be true, so when I got home I did a little research, mostly just so I could tell my friend to stop going around telling people that things are handmade when they just aren't . . . but that's not what happened. Here is what I learned.

Every stitch of crochet you have ever seen, every tablecloth, every curtain, every piece of lace trim or band on a hippy blouse at the Gap, everything was entirely and completely made by a human being exactly the way that you would do it if you were crocheting it yourself. Human, yarn, hook. That's it. The construction of crochet means that a machine can't do it, and hasn't ever yet. Just think about that. The tablecloth in the discount store? That's someone's work. Someone like you. Can you imagine how you'd feel if you made something like that, because I bloody well can, and if anyone told me it was worth anything less than their firstborn child and $1,000 I'd have exploded with rage. To see it at a discount store for sixty bucks—that's crazy.

Think about shopping for clothes. I was in a huge department store a little while ago. The kind where you can go into one of their stores in St. John's, Newfoundland, or Victoria, British Columbia, and you'll find exactly the same stock, and they had a whole raft of nightgowns with crochet trim. That's got to be thousands or millions of crochet bands, all the same, and no machine produced them. They all came from the hook of someone just like you who's earning a living churning the stuff out like it's noodles. In any honest estimation, these artists must be making pennies an hour to produce something that you and I would expect nothing short of a ticker-tape parade for accomplishing. Mentally add up how much crochet you've seen in your life, and then reframe it so you imagine a person making it. It's a mind blower. (If you have any room left in your brain, I'll give you this. Baskets are the same. All baskets. Every basket. True woven baskets are made by hand; machines don't make them. Toss that around in the old brain hopper the next time you're in Ikea and see how you feel.)

All crochet is handmade, the way you would make it. In a way, this makes me jealous of crocheters. A knitting machine was one of the heralds of the Industrial Revolution, created at the end of the 1500s. In the intervening eras, knitting machines have only become more complex, more efficient, and more incredible. I can go to the store right now and buy about twenty things that were knit by machine, and sometimes it will be obvious, like with scarves, hats, or mittens, where the "handknit" look is in vogue. Sometimes, though, only a handknitter himself would be able to spot the differences between what's available in the mass market and what's available as a special bonus for knowing me, or you. As a knitter, this essentially means that I can be replaced, but a crocheter cannot. I love the fabric knitting makes, and I prefer it to crochet. It simply suits me better. This means that I shouldn't feel an affinity for crochet, and I guess I don't, but I can't help but feel an affinity for whosoever made that tablecloth in the discount store. The one I made almost killed me, and I expect it to be cherished. The one she or he made is wrapped in plastic in Chinatown thousands of miles away, and most of the people looking at it don't even know what it is, never mind that the artist made pennies per hour to make it. Personally, I don't find crochet, in any incarnation, to be as beautiful as knitting, but there is absolutely no denying that it may have this one leg up on knitting. We as a civilization have imaged the human mind with magnetic resonance, obliterated diseases worldwide, built pyramids and the Internet, and traveled to the moon and even walked there . . . but we have never, ever figured out how to make a machine crochet, and that might mean that crochet is a far more human activity than is knitting.

THE DEEP DARK

*L*et me tell you a little something, a secret. I love getting up in the night, and I always have. I know that if you've got babies right now, you're probably going to have trouble believing that, but it's true. When my babies were little and woke me in the night, I got up with them, and but for the few nights when the sleep deprivation pushed me near the limits of survival, I loved it. The night has a lovely intimacy, and in the dark my baby and I were the only two people alive. I loved nursing them and rocking them and looking at their little fingers curled like unfurled moonflowers. (I know their father would tell you something different, that there were nights that I stood by the side of our bed with a screaming bundle of infuriated human and said, "You know, it's not like she and I are the only two people alive. You could get up and take a turn," but those were moments, not themes.)

The night has a certain sort of delicious loneliness. For those of us who like to be alone and find ourselves good company, but are beset by family and children all day, the night has opportunities. I know that if I stay up long enough, I'll be alone. It's a fetish that I indulge only occasionally as a married woman, since a pervasive desire to be alone can hurt the feelings of your spouse, but I'm writing this now, in the deep, dark quiet night, all alone, just my thoughts and me.

When I was a little girl, getting up in the night was understandably frowned upon, and even thwarted. My brother James was a serious nighthawk, and in being such, I think he had spoiled it for the rest of us. My mum still tells the story of him as a toddler, getting up in the night and wandering from his crib. Something woke her (likely instinct) and she discovered him standing on the stovetop in his plastic-footed jammies, trying to turn on the burners under cover of darkness. After that, the hallway had a strategically connived wall of empty apple juice cans set up as part barrier, part alarm, and any attempt to get by it toppled the cans and brought the fuzz down on you, even if you were just going to look out the front window to see how good your night vision was.

My fondest memory as a teen wasn't of a stolen kiss or a broken curfew (though technically, I got both) but of a walk in the night. I stole out my bedroom window and away with the boy next door. With my wool as my witness we got up to no big mischief but simply walked through the park in the night, through magic fog and mystic darkness. It is still the most romantic thing that has ever happened to me. I crept back in through my window that night, late and kissed, and with all my feelings about the luxury of the dark confirmed.

There is much to love in the night. I like that you can't see much, that things are secret and wild, unrevealed and insubstantial. Perhaps because my heart is that of a writer, I love that you can't see all of it. In the night, there are mysteries and uncertainties, and those empty spots where you aren't quite sure what's there are more than magical to me. The empty spots let me fill in the darkness myself. The night is like a coloring book; the lines are there, but the rest is up to me. You can wander or sit in the dark, writing stories about whatever may be in the gray spaces. There is more possibility in the dark.

As a grown-up, I still steal the nighttime moments where I can get them. I've always been near criminal when it comes to staying up too late. I love the hours after the family is asleep. My husband is in our bed, the girls are slumbering in theirs, so there are people here, but not really, and I am alone, but not really . . . and suddenly the world of possibility opens up in front of me. If I wake up in the night, I still get up and come downstairs, look out the window to test my night vision (it's not that great anymore), and let my mind wander and think. Sometimes I make tea, and sometimes I sit in the night and I knit.

Don't tell.

THE TIME OF THE BIG NOT KNITTING

I haven't always been a knitter, but I learned when I was four, so I don't really remember what it was like before I knit. Every now and then I'm on a bus or in a room with a bunch of other knitters, and I'll hear one say, "you know, I just don't know what I did before knitting," and they look genuinely perplexed. People who used to sit on the bus without knitting all the time now look at other humans doing just that, and their minds boggle at the possibility. How are those people doing that? Did I ever do that? How many hats could I have made in all those bus rides? While I don't know what I did before knitting, I understand the thoughts because I have a pretty good idea what I would do without knitting and, essentially, it can be summed up in two words. Poor behavior.

I would be unreasonable. I've often said that people only *think* I'm nice, or patient, or kind, and that really I'm no such things. My real personality is intolerant, impatient, judgmental, and possibly dangerous. It's like knitting surrounds me with some kind of science fiction bubble of kindness or patience that's activated by yarn. The minute that humanity or circumstance starts to bring out the worst in me, I flip the switch on my force field and zap! Personality reinforcements are generated around me. Forced to sit in a room with someone I find tiresome, annoying, or irritating, I have a choice. I can haul off and tell them that I think they've got the brain capacity of the hairball my cat hacked up and that their ideas have about the same content, or I can knit a row and calmly state, "I'm not sure I understand your premise." If one of my teens is screeching about how I can't possibly understand anything about her life and I'm ruining everything because raves are totally safe (it's just that I'm old and stupid), I can haul off and scream, "Of course I'm ruining your dangerous and demented plans. You have only sixteen years' experience on the planet, you think that nachos are a well-balanced meal, and that the guy with the ring in his nose is twenty-one years old and still in high school because he's 'deep!'" Or, I can knit a row and say, "I'm sorry, sweetie. I hear how upset you are, but you still can't go to a rave." Knitting while I wait for a doctor appointment is something to distract me from what I really want to do, which is stomp up to the receptionist and launch into a lecture about how my time is worth just as much as the doctor's is, and how I simply am not putting up with his policy of double booking anymore, and, as a matter of fact, I'll be revising his appointment book personally, right this minute, so that it shows some respect to the people who are supporting his career.

I knit when I worry, to help use up the time and space, and so that my vivid imagination doesn't add fuel to the fire. I knit when I'm stressed, to help keep the peace, and so that I don't make bad situations worse. In short, if I did not knit, I certainly wouldn't be married, and I wouldn't have friends, a job, or the ability to go out into public without slapping about twelve people a day—probably while drunk. Phrases like "a danger to herself and others" would be used, and, at the inquest, taking my knitting away from me would be cited as a major contributing factor to the "episode."

I have said it before, and I'll say it again. I do not knit. I am a knitter, and knitting is not something I do, it is a personality trait, and without my knitting, I would cope less well. (That's an understatement. When I say I would cope less well, I mean that I think about chewing on the legs of tables. Metal ones.) This, the fact that I use knitting for comfort, patience, help, and sanity, is understood really well by my family and friends—so well that when my children were toddlers they would bring me my knitting if I looked upset. So well that my girls, now that they are big, will, instead of saying, "I have bad news," will often precede a crappy report card or something else I won't like with the statement, "Mum, I think you might want to knit for this one." So well, that as I stood in my wedding dress, looking nervous, my friend Denny took my bouquet and replaced it with her knitting and asked if I wanted to "do a few lines to take the edge off." I am knitting. Knitting is me.

Knowing this about myself, it is difficult for me to imagine not knitting, especially by choice, so I was as shocked as anyone when that is exactly what happened. At the bleakest time of last year—if you live in a northern place you'll know this time, after all the leaves have fallen and been raked up but before the snow flies, when everything is gray and bare—my heart got broken.

It doesn't matter what happened. Hearts get broken all the time. Marriages crumble, people die, there are bad accidents, reversals of fortune, intentional hurts, crushing disappointments, or surprises that one can't bear. Every person is different, and to describe to you what broke my heart would only draw a divide between us. As humans we can't help it, can we? You hear about something that's a heartbreak to another human, and because you are strong where they are weak, you can't understand how it would hurt them. You can often see it in the face of someone as you try to explain your heartbreak. As you tell someone about something that has knocked you down, kicked you in the stomach, kept you awake and sobbing for ten nights, and then took your lunch money, you see that as sympathetic as they are to you, as much as they love you, they're sort of thinking, "That's it? That's what all this is about?" We're all different, and all you need to know is that something broke my heart, and

I was beyond sad—and most of my family went with me. The truth is that after years and years of being a remarkably blessed family, the forces that may be decided that it was our turn, and we got our share of hurt, disease, difficulty, and pain all in one go.

I cried. I cried in public, and really, I find crying in public so humiliating that I would rather be topless in a bar. (Okay, that's not true. Me and my forty-two-year-old breasts would be humiliated by that as well. I'm just trying to make a point.) I can't tell you of the hurt, and the sadness, and the way that I wondered if everyone I knew could ever be happy again, and the way that I envied people on the street who seemed happy to me. I barely ate. I scarcely spoke. I was comforted by my husband, friends, and family, but they were brokenhearted too, and it was a crappy system. I walked. I ran. I actually ran miles and miles, trying to outrun the hurt of it all. I ordered innumerable books on the topic of our hurt, but I didn't read many of them. Joe and I went to the grocery store and couldn't remember why we were there and ended up buying weird things we didn't need because we knew we were there for something, and, damn it, how can a box of baking soda not help?

There were days and days in a row when I coped by reaching for my compassion so far that the stretch burned, and days when I coped by finding the kindness in others. Some days I coped by ignoring everyone, screening calls, or sleeping. Some days I called friends or took long baths. What I didn't do was knit. Here I was, in one of the most trying circumstances of my life, and the thing that had always kept me sane didn't appeal at all. It was confusing and worrying. What did it mean that I didn't want to knit? Was I unraveling as a person? Was I still me?

I tried tempting myself with beautiful knits, the same way that one tempts the appetite of a person who's been ill. All their favorite foods, all their favorite drinks, all to entice them back on the road to health. I got out my favorite yarns. Beautiful, gorgeous things I'd been saving. When that didn't make me care about knitting, I went back to basics. Socks, hats, mittens—simple, good things—thinking that maybe if I started slow it would take hold again. I wasn't the only one working on it either. My family and friends kept giving me yarn, handing me knitting, waiting for it to work like it always had. I kept taking it from them too, holding the knitting, trying to make it work so I would feel better. It didn't work, though, and just as people feel ill at ease when a sick person won't eat, that's how upset we all were about the not knitting.

It's been a long time since then, and what I didn't know then, but I can speculate on now, is why I didn't want to knit. For starters, I *am* knitting. For lack of a better phrase, knitting is knit together into who I am, and coming back to knitting meant coming back to myself, and myself was such a crazy place to be right then that I didn't want to go there. I was sort of worried about being me. There was fear, and heartbreak, and indecision and a nightmare in which my normally effectual self was reduced to staggering around wondering with every breath if I was okay, or doing the right thing, making the right decisions, or even managing okay. Knitting would have been being myself, and I think it was only smart that I didn't want to be anywhere near that person and her responsibilities right then.

It also turned out, when I did try to knit, that it felt stupid. There was no way that you could take a situation in which everything was absolutely crazy and then sit there knitting. While usually knitting helped me feel better, this time it felt like fiddling while Rome burned. For the first time, I looked at knitting and felt like there was no real way that it could help. How, really, could I look at a problem as big as my problems were then and think that yarn would solve it? Was I out of my mind? Did I think that heartbreak could really be solved by merino? How would a simple skein of yarn solve it all? Would it help if I knit anyway?

The answer, of course, was no. In the face of a certain sort of tragedy, the lady sitting in the corner churning out a pair of socks looks crazy, and I could feel that it was crazy. Besides being solitary and meditative when what the time demanded was team effort and focus, it was also that knitting was, even when things are terrible, a comfort. It's a distraction, a way of not dwelling in the moment, or a way of stepping back a little so you can think.

For me, knitting is a huge coping mechanism, and it turns out there are times in our lives when it isn't right to be comforted or distracted. I'm not saying pain is good; I'm saying that I found that right then, when so many people were hurt, the best thing I could do was feel all the hurt and recognize that this was where I was, and that we would all live through it.

I've had people ask me, in my life, how I can listen and talk and knit, and I've always said that it is easy. Knitting doesn't take much of my attention at all. Despite the fact that it looks like a lot of my energy is somewhere else, that's not true, it's only the tiniest little bit of myself that's knitting—and besides (I've always told them) knitting has an effect on me. During this time, I realized that is very true. Knitting does have an effect on me, does help me disengage enough to cope, and does take up only a little, tiny bit of my energy. Most of the time I think that knitting helps me to pay attention. It reduces my urge to get up and wander, it gives me something to do with my hands, and far from being an indicator that I'm bored, knitting is often the way I'm keeping from being bored. Knitting takes the edge off what is difficult, challenging, or hurtful. Knitting forms that bubble around me, and in the circumstances that I suddenly found myself in, circumstances so awful, I realized that for me that bubble, that tiny bit of me that was given to knitting while I coped, wasn't working. It was almost disrespectful to knit. To pull myself out of that pain, to cushion it in any way with yarn and distraction, was a disservice to the very real hurt feelings of those around me. They deserved, and I deserved, to have me listening and talking with all the energy I could muster, and to be as engaged as I possibly could be. The significance of what was happening to us deserved exactly that amount of hurt, and to try and avoid any of it felt dishonorable, as though I were seeking to diminish it.

Gradually, a whole lot of the maxims that people said to us during the troubles (maxims that were infuriating when we heard them) turned out to be true. Time did heal a lot of wounds, we were strengthened by the difficulties, and we weren't given more than we could bear. Gradually, I came back to myself, back to a place where a little soothing was a good thing, and slowly then, I knit. I admit that at first I mostly just held my knitting, but as the burdens eased, my hands started to move. I started to knit, I stopped crying . . . and it was actually an inverse relationship. Knitting didn't seem to stop my tears, but the less I cried the more I was able to knit.

Washington Irving said, "There is a sacredness in tears. They are not the mark of weakness, but of power. . . . They are the messengers of overwhelming grief, and of unspeakable love." I will never know for sure what caused the time of the big not knitting. I won't know if it was the broken heart (mine, or someone else's) or if it was needing to do the work of grief without distraction, or even if I was just unwilling to leave that place and move on until it was finished somehow. I do know that there was a sacredness in my tears. They were necessary and unavoidable, and until I had cried the magic number of them, knitting was only going to get in the way. Once I had that sad work done, one by one my tears dried up, and one by one they were replaced by stitches on my needle, and I knit.

SNACKS

ere is the way you get yarn out of my stash: You tie one end of a rope to a doorknob, and the other end around your waist, tell a friend where you're going so they don't worry, and leave a note for your family telling them that you love them. Then you dive in and hope for the best, since you can't know how long you're going to be in there. I like to delude myself into believing that the stash has order, or some sort of organizing principle, but mostly I think I'm just telling myself that so that I don't have to try to figure out how to come up with an order or an organizing principle. It can be a little hairy in there, both literally and metaphorically. I do try to have it make some sense. If I have a whole bunch of a particular yarn, I bag it together for sweaters, and all those sweater bags are (mostly) in the same spot. The spinning stash is (mostly) not mixed in with yarn stash, and once last year when I was overwhelmed by a problem I couldn't sort out that was unrelated to knitting, I went on a rampage in there and put all the silk in one area. A similar urge a time before that put all the laceweight at least near each other, but I've since contaminated that by firing some stray yarn into there in an emergency that concerned itself more with getting things put away than putting things away in a sensible fashion. (Likely someone was coming over. I probably stuffed all that yarn in those bags moments after shoving the dirty dishes into the oven and after stuffing the dirty laundry in a closet while planning to wipe out the bathroom sink with a pair of tights from the floor. I may not be tidy, but I am bold.)

No matter what happens when I dive into the stash that way, there's one thing that I have to face up to. I have rather a lot of yarn in there that has no plan nor destiny, and occurs in really strange amounts. I speak here of the single skein phenomenon. I have a ton of single balls, skeins, and hanks that I really can't explain. There are skeins in my stash that are there because I simply thought they were pretty, or because they are souvenirs of places I've been, or knitters I met. (I refuse to be judged because of that. I used to think it was strange, until I met someone who buys a shot glass everywhere they go and lines them up on shelves in the family room. If they can do that, then I can do this.) There are other skeins that are samples, or stuff I was going to test to see if it felted nicely. There is even some yarn that I bought because I had a plan that made sense before I remembered that I'm not a supermodel, or yarn I own because I wish I looked better in blue than I do, and I keep buying it because hope springs eternal.

All of that yarn, though, has a purpose, as misguided as it may be, and I love it all. The single-skein phenomenon doesn't include any of that yarn. These are freestanding skeins that I have bought for . . . really no reason at all. I don't think they're going to be hats; there isn't enough yardage for socks; they aren't something I'm even planning to use as inspiration or a woolly desk ornament. They are there for no reason. None. I apparently bought them while I was in a trance state in a yarn shop—just picked each one up with no purpose at all, gave the shop my money, and walked out clutching another purposeless skein of yarn to add to the gajillions already at home. It's behavior that's entirely erratic and unmethodical, and while I admit to having a thousand weaknesses involving yarn, I like to believe that there is at least fleeting consideration given to my purchases. I might have a lot of yarn, but at the very least I want to be able to say it's there for a reason. The presence of these desultory skeins says that maybe that's not true. These yarns are there for no purpose, and I admit that I didn't even have one when I bought them. I worry sometimes when I think about this, that my relationship with yarn isn't healthy—or that it has hypnotic qualities or fumes that overcome me.

I was thinking about this a lot when I visited a friend who was on a diet. We were having coffee when her timer went off, and she got up, counted out twenty almonds, offered me the same, and then plunked back down. "Hungry?" I asked, confused about the timer.

"Not yet." she said. "It's a preemptive strike. If I have something now, before I'm hungry, then the theory is that I won't hoover down twenty-three cookies an hour from now."

"Good thinking," I agreed, and I accepted the almonds. Somewhere in the back of my mind, a light lit.

Preemptive eating seems like a fine strategy. It's a good way to avoid one of those episodes where you're starving, take temporary leave of your senses, and only recover in time to have a postmortem chat and debriefing about the appropriate role of chocolate in one's diet, or how wrong it is to eat whole cakes in single sittings. If you're never starving, then you won't ever eat like you are, at least theoretically. If you were trying to keep from eating a whole cake, I can see how a couple of strategically timed carrot sticks might take the edge off. All at once, I realized what's happening in the stash.

My self-control around food is rather good, but we all have our weaknesses, and my self-control around yarn is notoriously bad. Legendary, in fact. I've gone to a yarn shop with the absolute intention to buy nothing, and walked out twenty minutes later with a whole sweater's worth and the deflated feeling of having lost a little self-respect. I don't think there's anything wrong with buying yarn. I like buying yarn, but it should at least be intentional, and that's not what happens when you go in there and make snap decisions. It's impulsive and a little weak, and it's totally like deciding you're not going to eat any junk at a party and then lying in bed four hours later wondering what the hell you were doing when you stationed yourself by the chips and refused to give up the territory like it was a key holding in a world war. At first that's what bothered me about the single skeins in the stash. I thought that they were the result of those spasms in the yarn shops. I thought that I have all those hanging around because they're the symptoms of a yarn disease. I was looking at that stack of single skeins and feeling like they were the products of a yarn binge. I was wrong.

They are snacks. They aren't the disease; they're what I'm using as a treatment and prevention. It's like taking methadone instead of straight up using heroin—to draw a rather crass analogy. I can see what happened now. I was in the yarn shop, I started to get weak and feel a whole sweater's worth of yarn coming on, and I reached out for a carrot stick, the first little skein that I could find, and I bought it, and held it, and took it home. Those snack skeins are part of an instinctive protection plan. Without them, things could have been a lot worse, and that changed my attitude about them a little, made them more of a point of pride. They aren't random; they aren't there for no reason; and they might not have any intention of becoming mittens, but they're still serving a tidy little purpose. I'm okay with that, mostly. The only thing wrong with the system is that, just like other kinds of snacks, skeins can really add up.

THE COOL TABLE

When I was a teenager, I had a lot of problems. Not anything that was unusual or should put me in a category for special pity, you understand, just an ordinary list of problems that almost every teenager could come up with. I was dorky; I had trouble in a couple of subjects; I was short; I couldn't dance; I was lame at sports. I liked to read; I made some of my own clothes; my family had no money. While every other kid had a different but comparable list, my own personal list of adolescent problems was so intensely crippling that I really didn't see how they could ever stop defining my life.

Don't get me wrong—I had a lot going for me too. I was funny, I could be charming, and while I wasn't very pretty and had horribly big glasses, my figure was good, and I possessed a pretty big rack, which I'm ashamed to note, can make up for a lot if your primary audience is teenaged boys (who are more interested in breasts than glasses) and teenaged girls, who, while they resent that boys are more interested in breasts than glasses, know that it's a really unfortunate truth. I struggled through the way that most kids do, and the way I watch my kids struggle now. Things like skipping French because a boy you liked was skipping French and if you skipped French you could perhaps get a little face time with him, and knowing that's wrong and is going to mess you up later, but doing it anyway because you feel like the only thing that matters is now, even though you know that can't be true. How about worrying that the fact that you went to science with your fly undone and a piece of spinach in your teeth really was going to define your whole life, and feeling helpless to stop the humiliation anyway?

Every once in a while there was someone who didn't have problems in high school. Someone upon whom, for reasons that belong to the universe alone, some magical fairy dust had settled so that the Red Sea that was adolescence parted in front of them. They were the right size, the right shape, had the right grades, had the right sort of charm, dated the right people . . . burned small chickens by the willow tree at midnight on full moons. . . . I have no idea, but whatever mystic thing it is that you need to do to get through high school feeling like things are okay, these people had it. When I cast my mind back on those people who had it together back then, they're a pretty diverse group, and the unifying theme of them, the thing that they all had in common, wasn't how they looked or what they wore, or what clubs they belonged to, it was that they were comfortable—really, genuinely comfortable—being a teen and navigating high school.

Keep in mind that I'm not talking about the kids who looked like they were beautiful and in charge and had tons of friends, but were really only there because of some horrible power struggle that they conquered. You know the kind. The really pretty girl coasting through the school in tiny little $300 jeans, smiling away on the arm of some young Godly Adonis everyone adored (you know the one—the one who's fatal flaw was that he couldn't see that his girlfriends were all jean-clad harpies and barracudas who had the likes of me for breakfast without even thinking about it). I don't mean those girls, or those boys, because we all knew even then that they weren't actually happy, just powerful, and they worked a complicated system to be there, and we didn't really want to be them. We just wanted their jeans, and, actually, just wanted their jeans to fit. I'm talking instead about the kids who really were honest-to-goodness happy. The kids who had tons of friends, seemed to like everyone, and seemed to be liked by everyone. The ones who succeeded in one way or another at nearly everything that they set their hands to, and when they did fail, did so with humor and laughter that only further endeared them to all.

These were the kids who ended up being valedictorian and president of the student council and got awards for being community leaders. And when they got the awards, you actually clapped for them, because, while you were envious and wished that whatever it was that was working for them could for you,

you actually liked them, damn it, because they were likeable. I'm sure they've gone on to have their own problems and challenges, these civic leaders and volleyball captains and heads of the art club, but at the time, they looked like golden shining people. At lunch time, they sat in little knots of happy teenagers, and they laughed, and studied, and helped each other, and if you went up to them at their cool tables (because that's how I thought of them, cool kids sitting at a cool table) and talked to them, they were always nice. I have never, ever wished harder to be something more than I wished to be someone who was comfortable enough with themselves to be at the cool table.

Me, I was not that kid. I think I was born uncool. I was awkward and out of place from day one, right from that first afternoon in kindergarten when Julie let the water in the water play table out on Suzanne's velvet shoes and for the life of me I couldn't figure out why, or how, or if it was appropriate revenge for Suzanne showing off said shoes. (Julie is still my friend and has assured me that it was indeed appropriate, and that Suzanne was overly smug about her shoes.) From that moment, there has been a system at work, a series of credits and debits to whatever rank it is that determines who's cool and who's not, and despite spending a lot of time in my youth trying to figure that system out, probably as much as you did, I still don't understand. Lying in your bed at night wondering about the best way to say "hi" to someone the next day or whether or not you really did dare to show up in that shirt that your mum bought you that had the little ruffles on it, since that might or might not be the sort of thing that could ruin two weeks of good solid work on your image. I have never really had any idea how it works or if I'm doing okay, and it was particularly baffling in high school.

In high school, I tried to run the system. I really did. I noted that one of the cool kids wore her jean jacket inside out, and that everyone thought that was really, super cool, and so that night at home I stood in front of the mirror, jean jacket on inside out, staring in the mirror, and I realized that it wasn't going to work. I didn't have the secret, and while Marie could wear her jacket inside out, and whatever magic she possessed made her look like a creative person who wasn't afraid to let her inner self shine, me wearing mine inside out made me look like, at sixteen, I still didn't know how to dress myself and should be signed up for some special remedial help. I could see that. I really could, and it wasn't low self-esteem talking. It was that Marie could somehow walk into a room ten minutes late and make everyone else feel like they were early, and that's an adolescent voodoo that gets you to the cool table, and there's just nothing that anyone can do about that. It's the same voodoo that means that one kid can totally connect with a volleyball and send it over the net in a graceful arc to me (the kid with her knitting on the bench—just in case) waiting on the other side, and the ball, in a sort of cosmic destiny, has absolutely no choice but to follow its preordained path from the cool kid's hands to connect squarely (and much to the cool kid's horror) with my face. It's just the way it is, and nobody can fix it.

Once I figured that out, once I tripped on the stairs in front of the boy I liked and got a public nosebleed, once I tried to sew a skirt that looked like Lynne's and instead went to school swimming in a sea of denial and a travesty of fabric, once I showed off my plans for the school play's sets and got the gig, only to have my name accidentally left off of the program, once I essentially got the memo that this was definitely not my time, once I understood that being the sort of kid who wants to make her own yogurt and has a sizeable yarn stash while still in high school is just not going to be cool—ever—once I got that through my head (a volleyball to the face really can be an epiphany of sorts), it was almost freeing. I allowed myself to stop trying to be them; and for better or for worse, the only thing left to be was me.

I was just thinking, as I typed this, that if this were a novel for teenagers, one of those books with a lesson, or one of those movies that is supposed to make teenagers feel better about being a teenager, that this is the point where I would write about how I let go of trying to be someone else and embraced the real me, and in so doing, became loved by all. If Lindsay Lohan were in the story, that would be the resolution of the plot. She would have spent the whole film trying to be a cool girl—with tragic results for both her soul and her social standing—only to learn (tearfully) that, really, she should just be her herself, and then (ironically) she would be rewarded with the love of all, becoming the cool girl that she always wanted to be. (Actually, I think there is a Lindsay Lohan teenager movie like that. Actually, I think all teenager movies are like that.)

The reality is that it just doesn't work that way. Eventually all dorky, awkward kids realize that they can't stop the dork from happening, and they give up, and some of them outgrow it and become the sort of cool they always wanted to be, and some of them don't. Some of them actually become dorky, awkward adults who knit too much and have to tell people at parties that they "write knitting humor books" and endure the look that comes next. Some of those kids are never, ever going to be less dorky—never. For once, I would like to publicly state that, as someone who has endured a series of public humiliations that has continued since the day of the public nosebleed in grade nine. (In fact, I tripped over the doorjamb in the grocery store the other day only to discover my fly was down as people helped me up.) The great and glorious myth that we let Lindsay Lohan portray in movies is the absolute insanity that if you "be yourself" you'll somehow be cool. It pisses me off, because sometimes just being yourself doesn't pay off for a long, long time, and when you finally are yourself, whatever yourself is when you decide that's who you are, it doesn't necessarily pay off the way that the movies say it does.

Sometimes, when you finally are yourself—your knitting, yogurt-making, frumpily clad, not-too-tall, wearing-handknit-lace-shawls-in-the-grocery-store self—sometimes the payoff isn't what you think it is. Take me, just for example. I am unequivocally not less dorky than I was when I was that teenager. I still show up places and realize that I'm wearing all the wrong things, and I still find myself at parties where I am desperately out of place. Like the Christmas party I was invited to last year. I showed up wearing what I always do, which in my mind was something I thought was handmade and fantastic but was truthfully jeans and a T-shirt dressed up with a handknit shawl for a touch of class. The moment I arrived, I knew I was sunk. I'd brought a hostess gift of handknit scrubbies and pretty soap, and all the other families had a bottle of wine, and I wasn't just the only woman wearing a shawl, I was also pretty much the only woman not wearing a Vera Wang Christmas sweater with little sequined reindeer on it. I spent the whole evening doing that calculation that you do when you realize that you're in the wrong place and have to figure out how long you have to stay to not compound your dorkiness by being rude. When the family down the road left, so did I. Walking home through the dark, I asked myself important questions. Was my life always going to be like this? Was I ever going to be a woman comfortable with who she is? Why were Vera Wang sweaters so expensive?

I was crushed, and I stayed crushed until the next evening, when I went to a Christmas party at my local yarn shop. I walked in, wearing my shawl and my jeans, and I wasn't the only one. My friend thought my handknit gift was good, because she knit me something too. We told knitting jokes; we laughed together, an unlikely crew; and I stood there, surrounded by my people and I realized something. I'm sitting at the cool table. I've wanted to be cool my whole life, and here it had happened by accident. The things that once set me apart (like a big stash) are strengths in this place, and the things that were working for me then still are. (Except for the rack. Beauty fades.) Suddenly I'm sitting here with a lot of other people who the whole world might think are dorks, and even I can admit that I never thought the cool table would be in a yarn shop, but suddenly I feel like I imagine those happy kids did at their table in high school, and it might not be a movie plot, but it's more than enough.